Hou

COLES NOTES

Key Point

Basic concepts in point form.

Close Up

Additional hints, notes, tips or background information.

Watch Out!

Areas where problems frequently occur.

Quick Tip

Concise ideas to help you learn what you need to know.

Remember This!

Essential material for mastery of the topic.

COLES NOTES

How to . . .

Start Your Own Small Business

Planning & start-up

Financial backing

Marketing & sales

ABOUT COLES NOTES

COLES NOTES have been an indispensable aid to students on five continents since 1948.

COLES NOTES now offer titles on a wide range of general interest topics as well as traditional academic subject areas and individual literary works. All COLES NOTES are written by experts in their fields and reviewed for accuracy by independent authorities and the Coles Editorial Board.

COLES NOTES provide clear, concise explanations of their subject areas. Proper use of COLES NOTES will result in a broader understanding of the topic being studied. For academic subjects, Coles Notes are an invaluable aid for study, review and exam preparation. For literary works, COLES NOTES provide interesting interpretations and evaluations which supplement the text but are not intended as a substitute for reading the text itself. Use of the NOTES will serve not only to clarify the material being studied, but should enhance the reader's enjoyment of the topic.

COLES PUBLISHING. A division of Prospero Books
Toronto - Canada
Printed in Canada

Cataloguing in Publication Data

Kelly, Geoffrey M., 1946-

How to—start your own small business:
planning & start-up, financial backing, marketing & sales

(Coles notes) ISBN 0-7740-0592-0

1. New business enterprises. 2. Small business.
3. Entrepreneurship. I. Title. II. Series

HD62.5.K444 1998 658.1'1'41 C98-930643-7

Publisher: Nigel Berrisford
Editing by Paul Kropp Communications
Book design by Karen Petherick, Markham, Ontario
Layout by Richard Hunt

Manufactured by Webcom Limited
Cover finish: Webcom's Exclusive DURACOAT

Contents

CHAPTER ONE

The pros and cons of starting a small business

One of the great advantages of the free enterprise system is that individuals may take their own time, energy, skills and money, and start their own business. Something of value can be created which didn't exist before, or a service can be offered which is yours and yours alone. The success of these ventures depends greatly on the effort and intelligence you put in, the careful planning that must precede any start-up and the accuracy of your financial projections. When your business thrives, you can enjoy the benefits of your own labor both economically and personally. If the enterprise fails, at least you have the satisfaction of having tried your best to realize your own dreams.

People start their own businesses for a variety of reasons. Here are some common ones:

Tax benefits Owners of small businesses may deduct expenses incurred in the operation of their business from any income they receive. Often, this results in a significant tax savings. Remember, though, you need to make money before any deduction is worthwhile.

Setting your own schedule When you work for yourself, you have no one telling you to be somewhere at a particular time and you don't punch a time clock. The catch is that you do have to be self-disciplined to get any job done. Provided that you are self-disciplined, you can organize your daily schedule to your own advantage. You may be able to take time off work to spend time with your family, to travel or enjoy hobbies and pastimes. Owning your own business is the ultimate form of flex time.

Many home-business start-ups are being undertaken by men and women who find that flexibility in operating hours permits them to better look after young families. They trade off working late at night for the option of taking the kids to school and being home when the school day is done. Often, this is an excellent exchange.

Building equity for the future For many people this is a major reason for starting a business. Equity is another word for financial value and it is possible to create a large amount of equity in a small business over a few years. Those who work for others may retire with a pension, but have nothing else to show for years of hard work and dedication. If a business you start is successful, it may be sold to others or passed on to your children. A successful business can become a significant financial asset.

Creating your own job In this age of corporate restructuring and downsizing, many highly experienced people find themselves out of work. Sometimes it can be difficult to get a new job that duplicates the wages and benefits you received in your old job. Using your experience and previous contacts to start a business is a good way of creating a job for yourself. Sometimes independent work, such as consulting, can lead to earnings which exceed those made working for someone else.

Working out of the home means no commuting People who live in the suburbs or bedroom communities and commute to major cites to work know the expense and energy-drain commuting can become. Eliminating this aspect of a daily routine can be an incentive for many people to work from home. A one hour commute each way, every day, adds up to ten hours a week. If you don't have a company car this is a huge financial expense, and a tremendous loss of productive time. Since many small businesses begin at home, eliminating a commute provides both money and time which can be applied to your business.

Self-fulfillment Starting and operating a successful business can be a tremendous source of pride. Owning a successful business is also a way towards self-actualization that is seldom achieved by the average person.

Excitement The start-up of a business is a new beginning; it is always exciting. You get a chance to develop your own ideas and dreams. In large businesses many people are responsible for a specific area of business but never see the real results of their work; in a small business a single person may be responsible for a multitude of activities and your success is immediately apparent. If you start a small business you won't have to worry about being bored.

The three streams of small business

One metaphor for thinking about the realities of owning your own small business is to think of three "streams" making a "river" of business. Each stream is equally important to the success of your enterprise:

- **Operations** Your special service or product often gives the business its start-up excitement and takes up most of your time. But this is only one of three streams feeding the river.
- **Finances** Any company needs a supply of start-up cash, some sources for long-term financing and sufficient cash flow to keep going through tough periods. The primary cause of small business failure is inadequate financing.
- **Sales** You may have a wonderful product or service, but if no customers are beating a path to your door, your company can't make money. Often small companies are forced to make sales arrangements with agents, distributors and larger firms to make sure product goes out the door and profits come in.

BUT THERE IS A DOWNSIDE

While few people would expect that starting up a small business would be easy, many don't anticipate aspects of the work that can make it a real headache. Before you quit your day-job, make sure that independent work is really what you have in mind.

Working alone Some people really enjoy the social aspect of working in a business with other employees. The average person spends eight hours a day, five days a week at work in the company of their fellow employees. This includes taking coffee breaks together, chit-chat at the water cooler, lunches, company picnics, company organized sports and travel to other cities or even countries, as well as the normal interaction during the workday. Most people don't realize how many of their waking hours they spend with their co-workers. When you start a small business, it usually means that you work alone, at least until the venture begins to grow.

Hidden expenses Most employees don't understand how much it costs an employer to have a worker on the payroll. The conventional figures for the added cost of employees is 25 percent of gross salary or wages for non-union employees, and 40 percent for union employees. These cost are sometimes called "payroll burdens."

Self-employed people have to pay at least some of these costs themselves. All self-employed individuals have to pay Quebec Pension Plan, Canada Pension Plan and Employment Insurance premiums when they file their yearly tax return. These thousands of dollars sometimes come as a shock at tax-time.

An ironic twist of paying Employment Insurance via Revenue Canada is that a self-employed person may not collect it should the business go under. As well, self-employed persons may not claim for Workers Compensation if they are injured while at work. It is wise to purchase your own disability insurance if you become self-employed. As your own boss, you no longer have access to a company-paid benefit package. Fortunately, there are insurance companies that offer benefit packages to self-employed people that duplicate the disability, dental and medical coverage usually offered by large firms. But as a self-employed person, you have to pay for this insurance yourself - and it can be even more essential for you in a business that is dependent on your good health.

Severance When a large company downsizes or closes down, there is usually a severance package for affected employees. If you close your own business, there is no severance, and often nothing left in your bank account.

Vacations As an employee you were entitled to paid vacation; as an owner of a small business the cost of any time you take off comes out of your own pocket. Small business owners are notorious for forgetting that they deserve a holiday once in a while.

Risk The opportunity to succeed in a business is always offset by the possibility of going broke. Regardless of whether you set up your company as a proprietorship, a small company or a corporation, there's going to be a fair amount of your money and a great deal of your hopes and dreams in the operation. As one business phrase goes, "Sooner or later, every small businessman has to be willing to bet his house on the business." Not every bet comes in a winner.

Legal liability It is an unfortunate fact that many people in business resort to litigation to solve problems. There are ways to protect yourself against law suits or at least to minimize their impact on your business, but every enterprise comes encumbered with legal liability.

Income variation All businesses have fluctuations in cash flow and profit. Some years are bumper years, some years are bust years, and most years fall somewhere in between. Unlike an employee who can rely on a steady flow of wages, a small business owner may have to adjust his spending according to the vagaries of the market. It often takes years before there's enough cash in the bank to weather a serious business storm.

Paperwork All businesses are highly regulated by governments, some more than others. The paperwork associated with this regulation is hard to swallow when you realize it is costing you money and time. The wise small business owner will accept this inevitability and figure the cost of this work, and the time to do it, into schedules and routines. It's just a cost of doing business.

These cautions are not meant to discourage you from starting your own business, but to point out the reality of the business world. Difficulties in business start-up and operations should not be perceived as insurmountable problems, but as situations to be resolved. It is amazing how many early problems turn out to be later opportunities.

IS OWNING YOUR OWN SMALL BUSINESS FOR YOU?

The final decision on whether or not to go into business is a personal one. The chart below suggests some of the character traits that will indicate whether you possess the personal attributes to make a success of your own business.

Ten questions before your start your own business

- ❑ Am I a self-starter?
- ❑ Can I handle many different tasks at the same time?
- ❑ Do I have self-confidence and drive?
- ❑ Do I know how to set goals and stick with them?
- ❑ Am I a risk taker?
- ❑ Am I self-disciplined?
- ❑ Am I a problem solver?
- ❑ Am I a "people" person?
- ❑ Do I like to be organized and make decisions?
- ❑ Am I a "business-oriented" person?

If you answered "yes" to a majority of these questions, you have many character traits that will be helpful to you when and if you start a business. If you answered "no" to a majority of the questions, you may wish to do some soul-searching as to whether you would really enjoy the challenge of owning and operating your own business.

CHAPTER TWO

What kind of business could you start?

The decision on which kind of business to operate is an exciting process. Probably the most important factor in choosing a business is whether or not you believe in the product, idea or service you are considering. This enthusiasm will go a long way towards the eventual success or failure of your enterprise, especially if and when the going gets tough.

> Do yourself a favor - if you are going to start a small business, start something that you like to do.

Most people have a special knack, experience, hobby, trade or skill that can be developed into a small business. Sometimes this special quality has become evident at work, sometimes as a hobby, sometimes it's a goal you've had since childhood. Chances are you already have a vague concept of the kind of business you'd like to set up. This list will suggest a few types of small businesses where your concept can be turned into a real enterprise.

Consulting A consultant is someone who has a special expertise in a particular area and who provides this expertise to companies for a fee. Many companies retain former employees as consultants. This allows them to use the consultant on an as-needed basis. It also allows the consultant to pick and choose assignments.

Some people who have lost their jobs due to downsizing and corporate restructuring have been rehired as consultants to their previous employer, or have used their previous work experience to consult to other companies in the same industry. If you work for a company that is considering downsizing their workforce, it is a good idea to pre-empt the inevitable. Be ready to present a proposal to the owners so they might find it beneficial to retain you as a part-time consultant. From there, you can branch out into other related areas. Many successful consulting companies have been started this way.

If you are laid-off and rehired as a consultant to avoid the cost of having you on the payroll, be prepared for trouble from Revenue Canada. The rules for hiring former employees as consultants change regularly, but two common restrictions are constant: as a consultant (or independent contractor) you *must* have more than one client and you *must* provide your own equipment. You should consult a lawyer and/or accountant if you are setting up a business as a consultant and your former employer is a client.

As a tradesperson Many businesses are started by people who have served an apprenticeship, become a journey-person and worked for a company as a skilled worker for a number of years. These people may have accumulated the necessary experience and equipment to do their job independently, and it is a small jump to become a self-employed small business owner. Provided that a steady flow of work can be found, and that an appropriate amount of time is devoted to the administrative side of the business, this is an excellent way to get started.

Hobbies and crafts Some hobbies can lead to an expertise that can be easily converted into a business venture. Some examples of hobbies that people have developed into small businesses include photography, music, woodworking, fishing, fly tying, sailing, weaving, camping, sewing, pets, public speaking, auto repair, furniture re-finishing and dozens of other pursuits.

Even if there is little work directly possible in the area of your hobby, try to think about ancillary areas. All hobbies and crafts use supplies, and the supplying of crafts-people or hobbyists is a major business. Think about where you receive your supplies and services for your hobby or craft, and then consider whether or not there is a need you could fill. There may be a business waiting to happen.

If anyone has ever offered to pay you for your handicraft or the product of a hobby, this is a major tip-off that you may have a viable business at your fingertips

Selling If someone manufactures a product, someone else must sell it. Companies who cannot afford full-time sales people use agents. Agents often sell the same type of product for a number of different companies. A sales agent is therefore is a self-employed business person. If you can convince one manufacturer to give you his product to sell, you can then build on this and get the rights to other manufacturers' products. It's best to keep your product line in the same category of merchandise and within the same territory. One very big advantage sales agents enjoy is that they do not bear the cost of inventory. You simply get paid a commission on your sales and the company bears the burden of inventory, shipping and cash collection.

Services The service industry exists because there is a need by people to have others supply expertise, equipment and facilities to fulfill a need. This is the largest growth area in business today. Each major sector of industry in the economy has a service aspect to it, and some of these can be performed by an independent business person. Consider the following industries and a few of the service businesses that are related to them:

AUTOMOTIVE

detailing	mufflers	painting	oil change
tune-ups	salvage	tinting	storage
restoring	accessories	tires	audio systems
washing	parking	leasing	rust-proofing
customizing	alarms	upholstery	shocks

HOUSING		
carpet cleaning	re-siding	landscaping
window cleaning	renovations	furnace maintenance
house cleaning	pool maintenance	duct cleaning
roofing	driveway paving	gardening
eavestroughing	drain unplugging	deck building
painting	decorating	greenhouses
gazebos	Venetian blind cleaning	wiring

PERSONAL CARE		
shopping	hair care	personal development
voice training	dieting	manicure
telephone answering	baby sitting	geriatric care
home nursing	fitness training	home schooling
language courses	formal wear	

BOATING		
storing	shipping	delivering
repairing	painting	restoring
engine maintenance	launching	mooring
building	sail-making	towing

COMPUTERS		
upgrading	repair	training
desktop-publishing	Web sites	programming
building	program modification	selling

Entrepreneurship Entrepreneurs are people who perceive a business opportunity and put all the parts together to make it work. In one sense, all small business people are entrepreneurs, however there is a special breed of entrepreneurs who might better be described as facilitators. These are individuals whose basic skills are in business administration. They may possess no knowledge or skill in a particular area, but they understand exactly who they need to help them achieve a goal. If they need an engineer, they will hire one; if they need a "numbers" person they will hire an accountant; if they need an object designed, they will hire an appropriate person. This type of entrepreneur acts as a conductor of the business "orchestra."

INVESTIGATING OTHER BUSINESS OPPORTUNITIES

If you are considering starting a specific business, it may be advantageous to attend an industry-specific trade show. You will be able to meet your potential competitors and possibly make some business contacts. Trade shows are common in the automotive, sporting, boating, home, publishing and construction fields. A check in the *Globe and Mail* or on the Internet will reveal many more.

Franchises

A franchise is the opportunity to be an owner of a business operation within a large corporation. For this opportunity, you pay a fee and agree to abide by the rules and regulations of the corporation. The advantage is that all the leg work to ensure a profitable business has been tried and tested. Franchise corporations may offer training, advice and products to the owners of individual franchises. Additionally, franchisees of large national organizations benefit from collective advertising - the kind that gets the name out in front of the public through mass market advertising. All of this comes at a price of course, and the most profitable franchises are often the most expensive to buy.

Although buying a franchise removes some of the uncertainty of success, it also removes the challenge and subsequent fulfillment of starting, owning and operating your own business from scratch.

One caution about franchises: some companies are not completely honest about the profitability and work involved in running the franchises they sell. Investigate carefully before you begin investing tens of thousands of dollars. Check with current franchise owners, read the prospectus carefully, get legal assistance, make sure you'll have operating funds left after paying for the franchise. For every McDonald's millionaire franchisee, there are five people who have lost thousands on a fly-by-night franchise operation.

One simple place to get ideas to start your own business is the Yellow Pages. Another is the classified section and business section of your local paper. Your local bookstore will have a whole section devoted to business and you will find books solely dedicated to ideas for new businesses. There are also directories of businesses at your local library, and these listings may give you an idea for a business that you may not have thought of.

Many industries have trade publications specific to their industry, and if you are gravitating to one particular industry it may be useful to obtain these publications. Large city libraries subscribe to every trade paper published, therefore you may save the cost of the subscription, by spending some time at the library looking through these publications.

These ideas are only the tip of the iceberg. There are literally thousands or perhaps hundreds of thousands of ways of going into business. You may be able to think up an entirely new business or a new twist on an old idea.

Buying an existing business

You may consider buying an existing business rather than starting one from scratch. There are many advantages to doing this and a few cautions.

Advantages

- You avoid the uncertainty of starting a new enterprise.
- It's a fast way to start a business.
- Profit will be available sooner than if you start your own business.
- A poorly run business may be purchased at a relatively low price and your efforts can increase profits.
- It may be easier to borrow money on an existing business since the lender can review the track record of the business.
- It is common for sellers of businesses to finance some of the purchase price. Some sellers might find it beneficial from a tax point of view to take payment for a business over a number of years.
- There may be existing credit arrangements that can be assumed by a subsequent owner.
- Some purchase agreements allow for the previous owner to stay on for a specified period to train the new owner in the operation of the business.
- Some businesses may have trained staff who wish to continue with a new owner.
- Many of the questions of viability are answered when you buy an existing business.

Disadvantages

- You pay for the past efforts of others.
- Some businesses rely on the specific input of the creator of the business; when a successor takes over some, businesses do not do as well as they did under the previous owner.
- Buying an existing business is complicated and should only be pursued with the advice of a lawyer and an accountant.
- The location and leases are predetermined and may restrict growth later.
- You pay for an intangible called "goodwill." This a value placed on the reputation and customer base of the business by the owner. If you start your own business you create this value yourself.

- There is a chance that you may buy a business, and no matter how much expert advice you receive, you may discover hidden flaws that eventually lead to problems.
- You may inherit pre-existing legal problems with a business.

No matter which business you choose to start, remember, the level of success you achieve will be directly proportionate to the amount of effort you put into it. Hard-working business owners create their own luck.

Test your concept

One of the most effective ways to test your business plan is to present it to yourself. Before you go out and try to convince a bank to loan you money or your brother-in-law to invest, make sure that you would actually invest in your concept. Listen to your own voice as you put forward the proposal, look over the supporting paperwork, and then ask: "If a friend came to me with this proposal, would I put my money behind it?" If your honest answer is no, don't waste your initial efforts on others until you've fixed up your business plan.

CHAPTER THREE

Legal issues you'll need to know

Among the first decisions you'll have to make in setting up your own small business is the type of ownership which will work best for you. The two most common kinds of ownership when starting a small business are sole proprietorship and partnership. Although there may be exceptional cases when a more complex form of ownership is required, the benefits of limited and incorporated forms of ownership are usually not appropriate when starting a small business. Information regarding these types of ownership are included here to enhance your general knowledge of business options.

SOLE PROPRIETORSHIP

Sole proprietorship describes a business which is owned lock, stock and barrel by one person. The advantage of sole proprietorship is that it is the easiest and cheapest way to own a business. Decide on a name, print up some stationary, business cards and invoices - and you're in business. Often, this is the best organization for small, part-time enterprises which will simply supplement the family income.

For tax purposes, the income from a business held as a sole proprietorship is the same as personal income. After expenses, the income is taxed at personal income tax rates and is always taxed in the year it is received. This may be a disadvantage or an advantage depending on a person's other sources of income and the changing rules of Revenue Canada. An accountant or lawyer can advise on this matter.

A disadvantage of a sole proprietorship is that the owner is personally responsible for the liabilities of the business. This includes loans, debts and the result of any successful lawsuits against the business. As well, all income must be reported in the year it's received, so there is no way to spread income over a number of years.

Of course, the most positive thing about sole proprietorship is that the owner gets to make all the decisions and thereby reap all the rewards from any resulting success. Another attraction of sole proprietorship is that it is the least-regulated form of business ownership.

PARTNERSHIP

A partnership is a business owned by two or more individuals. The regulation and set-up of a partnership is the same as a sole proprietorship - profit or loss is divided according to the contribution of each partner. The portion of profit taken by each partner becomes part of their personal income and is taxed accordingly. The partnership, itself, pays no taxes.

Unless stated otherwise in the partnership agreement, each partner may legally bind the business; so trust is vitally important. Each partner is also legally responsible for the *total* liabilities of the business. Since the actions of each partner affect the other partners, it is wise to have a partnership agreement before the business begins operation. Some items in a partnership agreement might include: how much money each partner is investing, how the profits will be divided, whether or not a partner may sign contracts or other legal documents independently, how many signatures are required on cheques and how much work each partner will do.

The relationship of partners in a legal partnership can be complex and it is essential to retain a lawyer who will draw up a partnership agreement. Business partnerships are notorious for disputes amongst the owners. A partnership agreement will at least provide a reference for resolving misunderstandings.

There are many good reasons for entering into a partnership, both for business management and for raising capital. Some people find it too lonely at the top; they need someone with whom to share their dreams and aspirations. Partners can bring talents and skills which are unavailable to a single owner. Partners may also provide a convenient source of investment funds unavailable to sole proprietors. The disadvantage to all this, of course, is that you have to get along well with your partners. A serious falling-out can lead to dissolution of your company, and rarely on terms that you'll find fair.

LIMITED COMPANY OR CORPORATION

A limited company, also called a corporation, is a legal entity which may be regarded as a separate entity from its owners. The owners of a limited company are called shareholders. The shareholders elect directors (usually from amongst themselves) who are responsible for the operation of the business. A limited company must pay income taxes on its profits separate from the income of the shareholders. Shareholders of a limited company may receive dividends at the discretion of the directors. Corporations are also required to file annual reports.

In the past, it was said that directors could limit their liability for the actions of the corporation, but this is not completely true especially in areas of taxes, worker safety, employee payroll contributions and environmental issues. The protection of directors regarding the financial liability of a limited company (since liability of a corporation is limited to the assets of the company), is reduced by the fact that most financing of new businesses requires a personal guarantee regardless of the legal status of the company. This means you may still have to mortgage your house to get bank financing even if your company is legally incorporated. Corporations are registered provincially by the Department of Consumer and Corporate Affairs and federally by Industry Canada.

The bottom line

What does it cost to set up a company legally?

- Sole proprietorship: $0 to $100, not including other business costs
- Partnerships: $500 to $2000 for initial legal work, little thereafter
- Corporations: $2000 to $5000 for initial legal work, $500 to $2000 each subsequent year to file documents and annual reports

Numbered companies

The naming of corporations is somewhat more complicated, time-consuming and costly than for sole proprietorships or partnerships, therefore, some businesses incorporate under a number which is assigned by the government, e.g. 123435 Ontario, Ltd. If these companies wish to use a normal sounding name for their business on letterhead and signs, they use a trade name which is registered with the appropriate government agency. This form of a corporation is most popular in the real estate sector.

Naming your company

Naming your company is an important part of starting a business. It is also a creative and enjoyable exercise. The name of your business may tell customers something about what you do and can give your company a distinctive flavor. Note the different flavor of Joe's Heating compared to WarmAir, Cozy Heating or Prestige Heating and Cooling, Inc. There are consultants who advise specifically on company and product names. Even if your name search is limited to a brainstorming session with friends, think carefully before you begin laying out big money for stationery.

Here are a few points to consider when picking a name for your business:

- Don't try to name a company so that it appears first in the yellow pages.
- Avoid a name that will become outdated quickly
- Choose a name that is easy to pronounce and spell.
- Long names are harder to remember than short names.
- Pick a name that indicates the nature of your business.
- Try to pick a name that distinguishes your business from others.
- Using your first name for your business sends a message that you are operating a one-person show.

REGISTERING THE NAME OF YOUR BUSINESS

It is possible to operate a business as a sole proprietorship or partnership without registering the company name, especially if it is simply a modification of your own name. No one else can say that Robert Q. Jones Consulting is infringing on their business so long as your name is Robert Q. Jones. But if your company becomes hugely successful, someone may register the name of your company and force you to buy back the name or prevent you from operating under that name. Conversely, another company may already be using the name you've chosen. In that case, your use of it may expose you to a lawsuit and ultimately force you to change the name of your company - and pay damages as well. Finally, a bank usually requires a business name to be registered before they will open a business account.

The registration of businesses and business names is done by the appropriate provincial ministries in each province. The process is simple: go to the ministry that governs business registration, line up, pay the fee and your company is registered. The fee for registration is minimal. This is a simple process and the services of a lawyer are not necessary. If you do not wish to go through the process, some law firms retain a paralegal service who will do the lining up and paper work at the registry for a small fee.

Many people believe the name they choose for their business is unique; in reality, most names or similar names are already being used. It is therefore usual to submit alternate choices when applying to register the name of a business. If your first choice is taken, any one of your choices may be used, therefore make sure the alternate names are as good as your first choice. If you are concerned about any conflicts in the name of your business, there are firms which will do a name search and some government ministries will do a limited name search for a fee when you register your business.

TRADEMARKS, COPYRIGHT AND PATENTS

Another way of creating a unique identity for your company is to create and register a unique trademark. A trademark may be a logo, a word, a symbol, a phrase or package design. A unique combination of these is also a trademark. Although it is not mandatory to register a trademark, it may be advisable to do so if your trademark is an important part of your business identity. If you use a trademark without registering it, you may have to fight for that right later in court. A lawyer or a trademark agent who specializes in trademark registration is the best person to do this work for you.

If you are on a shoestring budget when starting your small business, it may be wise to forego the expense of using a trademark until the volume of business warrants the expense of registering one. Trademarks are registered under the Trade Marks Act which is administered by Industry Canada. You may obtain free literature from Industry Canada on the details of trademark use and registration.

Copyright is the exclusive right of owners of original creations - music, literature, artwork, photographs, videos, movies, reference works or computer software - to reproduce their work for money. Owners of copyrights may permit others to reproduce a work, but usually for a fee. Copyright lasts the lifetime of the creator plus fifty years, therefore copyrights can become important assets in a person's estate.

Copyright is not automatic when an original work is created. Although registration is not compulsory, it is advisable if a large part of your business relies on copyrighted work. A lawyer who specializes in copyright protection will guide you through the complexities of registration. Industry Canada supervises copyright registration in Canada. Registered copyright makes the sale of copyrighted works easier and provides the basis for the defense of copyright infringement.

The importance of copyright is illustrated by the story of Richard Berry who wrote the Rock n' Roll classic "Louie Louie." He sold the rights to the song in 1956 for $750. Every time a band records "Louie Louie" they must pay the current copyright holder a fee, likewise when a radio station plays any version of the song. The total revenues of "Louie Louie" over the years have totaled in the tens of millions of dollars, but Mr. Berry got nothing beyond his original $750.

If you create a new product or process, you may protect your investment by registering a patent. Patents are registered with Industry Canada and protect the inventor from others copying, manufacturing or selling the invention for a period of twenty years. Patent registration is a long and expensive procedure; it may be wise to obtain the services of a lawyer who specializes in patent registration or a patent agent.

REMITTING TAXES

GST Businesses that do a certain amount of volume are required to register and collect Goods and Services Tax. The level of business volume below which GST is not required to be collected may vary according to changes in the legislation, but currently is set at $30,000. If you do not collect GST from start-up, be prepared to use your own money to pay it when you are required to file a GST return.

GST calculations for collecting the tax vary from business to business. An accountant can advise which method to use for your type of business. There are also different calculations for the submission of the GST. The "quick method" uses a formula to calculate the amount payable from the amount collected; the long method subtracts the GST your business pays for goods and services from the GST it collects from customers. Ask your accountant which formula is best for your business. This is one place where an accountant can not only justify his fee, but increase the profit of a small business by helping you avoid excessive tax payment.

Unless your business has a large volume of cash at start-up, apply for a yearly, rather than quarterly payment of the GST. This will save time and money in accounting and bookkeeping costs. It also lets you hold on to GST received for a longer period of time.

PST Depending on the province you operate in, and if you sell goods directly to the public, you may be required to collect Provincial Sales Tax - PST. As with GST, an accountant will be able give you the best advice on the collection and submission of PST. The government also provides assistance with booklets and through phone consultation.

Income tax It is natural for owners of small businesses to resent the portion of their income that goes to the federal government at income tax time. On the other hand if you pay a lot of tax, it means you had a lot of income. The best way to minimize tax is to keep good records and rely on an accountant to give you the benefit of any deductions possible. The best way to avoid a hefty tax bill in April is to remit quarterly tax payments based, not just on what the government requires, but on what you will probably owe.

While it is unusual for the government to prosecute *individuals* for minor amounts of tax evasion, the relationship between the government and small business is quite different. The government can be quite aggressive if they suspect a business of tax evasion. Tax evasion is a serious offense and it is not worth the grief it can inflict on you and your business. Be sure you know where the line between evasion and avoidance lies. Consult your accountant and lawyer if you have any doubts on this matter.

LICENSES AND REGULATIONS

The licensing requirements for businesses vary from industry to industry and from locale to locale. Certainly the list of licenses and permits is too long to explore here, so a lawyer is the best source of information. If you wish to research this yourself, you may find the local Chamber of Commerce, municipal, provincial or federal officials quite helpful.

Generally speaking, you can operate a home office out of your house without violating residential zoning regulations, but if you're doing auto repair or catering or steel fabricating, then you'd better check local zoning and business regulations quite carefully.

If your business is located in a commercial or industrial property you will have to apply for a license to operate from the municipality. Part of this application will confirm that the zoning of the property suits your type of business. Applying for and obtaining a license to operate a business in a municipality will result in a small bill for business tax.

As with licenses, regulations vary with place and type of business. Here are a few of the common ones you may encounter:

- The Building Department of your local municipality - the Building Code
- The local fire department - the Fire Code
- The Health Department - health regulations
- The Department of Labor - Occupational Health and Safety Act
- Worker's Compensation Board - Workers' Compensation Act
- The Department of the Environment - hazardous materials legislation

DO YOU NEED A LAWYER FOR ALL THIS?

If your small business is a part-time consulting operation from your house, you may well be able to set up and operate your company without legal advice. But the larger and more ambitious your business plan, the more likely you are to need a lawyer.

If you are required to sign a contract or a partnership agreement to start your business, a lawyer is essential. If you know someone in business whose opinion you respect, ask them to recommend a lawyer. When choosing a lawyer note that most lawyers specialize. A lawyer suitable for a small business will be an expert on small business regulations, small claims litigation, tax rules as they relate to small businesses and investment opportunities tailored for small business. The key words here are "small business." Lawyers who specialize in corporate law, family law or criminal law may not be a good choice for a small business owner. The ultimate test of the suitability of a lawyer is whether or not they have other small business owners as clients, and whether these clients are happy with the service they receive.

If you are starting a sole proprietorship you may not need a lawyer immediately, but when your business begins to grow it is wise to retain a lawyer. Ultimately all businesses need legal services: there may be contracts or leases to sign, collections to make, lawsuits to file or future decisions to incorporate your company. Since most lawyers do not charge for an initial consultation, it is possible to shop around before deciding who will represent your business. Legal fees are only charged for work done, therefore there is no cost in having a lawyer available to respond to legal issues. Some lawyers will say after a consultation "Do you wish to retain me?" If the answer is yes, they may require the payment of a retainer - a lump sum to be held in their account and used up as you require work to be done. This usually means you have some work for them to start on immediately. Once you have developed a relationship with your lawyer a retainer should be unnecessary.

Sadly, the first encounter many small business owners have with lawyers is when they are involved in a lawsuit. A lawsuit occurs when a dispute between two parties cannot be resolved and one of the parties files a claim with a court to recover damages. The other party may defend the action by filing a counter claim. No matter the amount of the claim involved, lawsuits are expensive to a small business both in terms of time and finance. Sometimes a little legal advice at the outset can prevent such problems later on.

Don't just rely on a book

The advice in this book - or any book you read about small business - has real limitations. Laws and regulations pertaining to any business can change with each new sitting of the legistature, so any written advice is quickly out of date. Banking policies change with regulation and competition, so may be very different by the time you're starting your business. Government assistance programs, employment practices and business opportunities differ from town to town, province to province. For all these reason, you need professional help. Advice from a lawyer and an accountant is **essential** for start-up, and you may well need additional professional advice as your business begins to gear up.

CHAPTER FOUR

Where to get help for start-up

One of the biggest mistakes people make when starting up their first business is the assumption that they already "know cnough" and will somchow bc ablc to "go it alonc." This is simply never true. One of the real advantages of a business partnership is that there is at least one other person to provide information, test out ideas, and make sure that a particular idea is sound before thousands of dollars are spent in development.

A sole proprietor must also realize that he or she needs help. Some of it will be professional - lawyers, accountants, government officials. Some of it will be related more directly to the business - bankers, financial advisors, colleagues and associates who know the product or service. And some of it will come from the larger community - your suppliers, customers and clients.

Fortunately, help is not hard to find. And not everyone who can provide valuable information to your company has to be paid for their wisdom. Here are some sources for valuable information and contacts.

NETWORKING

Networking is simply a matter of meeting and developing 8 business contacts. This is important to any business, no matter the size, but essential to small businesses, especially one-person operations. Networking allows a business owner to expose the company product or service to the marketplace. It also allows a small business owner to learn about resources such as suppliers or services that can be beneficial to their own business. Here are some places to network.

Breakfast clubs are specifically set up so that small business people can network. Be prepared to attend these very early in the morning since business people need to finish their meetings before the main business day begins. The basic premise of a breakfast club is that everyone knows something which may be beneficial to someone else. Sales leads or business tips are exchanged at breakfast meetings. Some clubs require the participants to offer one idea, tip nor lead at each meeting. This need not be an earth shattering idea, perhaps just a cost-saving tip on leasing office equipment. You can also pass out business cards and brochures and receive the same from the other participants.

Associations Many businesses have industry-specific associations that represent the interests of the group. Associations might keep their members up to speed on the latest legislation affecting their business, or advise their members on training courses and grants. As a member of an industry-specific association you will at least get to know your competitors. The prestige that comes with membership in an association may also be used in promotional material.

Tools of the trade

Business cards are an inexpensive and effective way of getting your own name and the name of your company publicized. If cost is a consideration, large business supply stores offer inexpensive business cards printed on the spot. Alternately, you may purchase a software program for your computer that will make it easy to print business cards.

Always carry an adequate supply of business cards when you are out and about, either socially or on business. Your business card is the cheapest but most essential form of advertising.

OFFICIAL SOURCES

Government is an important source of information, assistance and business. Government bookstores publish many titles that relate to the operation of small businesses. (Some are free; others must be purchased.) There are also advisory programs for small businesses financed by the government. A phone call to your local, federal or provincial business development office will open up a pathway to many valuable resources. Remember it's your taxes that pay for this information and these services, so you really ought to make use of them.

Chambers of Commerce and **Boards of Trade** are excellent places to meet business contacts. They are operated by members of the business community, and represent business interests to the community and government. Many of their events are open to non-members.

The Public Library offers many services to owners of small business. In major centers, they carry all the latest trade magazines, have files of information on companies in the community and across Canada, and sometimes offer Internet research services. "Deposit" libraries also have copies of governmental regulations, Statistics Canada reports and government documents that might impact on your business.

COMMERCIAL SOURCES

There are companies whose principal business is to provide information to other businesses, either at start up or while they are operating. Some businesses you might find helpful are in market research, advertising, display, printing, accounting and law. There are even companies that sell sales leads to other companies. Depending on the nature of your business, it may be well worth it to pay for professional advice or services. When a small business retains the services of business consulting firms, they are in effect buying not only advice and information, but access to the consultant's contacts.

Mailing lists are lists of customers' names, addresses and phone numbers which are used to optimize a promotional advertising campaign. They may be produced by a company or organization through the normal day-to-day business and then resold to other companies.

Companies also use their own accumulated mailing list to send out regular sales information to their customers. You may produce your own mailing list quickly by placing a special offer advertisement in a newspaper which asks customers to fill out a coupon to receive a discount. Mailing lists may also be purchased from groups such as universities, magazines or department stores.

How small can you start?

There are many business advisors who would say it's impossible to start up a small business with less than $100,000 in capital. Of course, every entrepreneur knows that Steve Jobs started Apple Computers with far less, or has heard just how cheap the early McDonald's franchises used to be. Small-scale, part-time businesses don't require a fortune to start up, but they do need the basics:

- **a filing cabinet** – because computers often fail and paperwork is essential
- **a separate phone line** – because you don't want your kids taking business calls
- **business cards and stationery** – because you don't want your small company to *look* small
- **enough money to keep going for 18 months** – this can be from other employment or from cash in the bank, but the break-even point always takes 50 percent to 100 percent longer to reach than you could possibly expect

CHAPTER FIVE

Small business finance

One definition of business is this: a profit-making activity that fulfills the needs of people for goods or services. Note the important word "profit-making." An owner of a business always expects a return on investment in the form of profit on goods and services provided. Simply stated, the goal of business is to produce a profit. The supplying of goods or services and the resulting payment by a customer is called a business **transaction**. It results in **cash flow**, which is an important sign of business health, but the bottom line of any business is whether or not it can make a **profit**.

RECORD KEEPING

The kinds of financial records required by your small business will vary according to the nature of the enterprise and the volume of business activity. These records show how much money is coming into your business and how much is going out. They will also allow you to analyze how efficiently your business is operating and flag problems if they develop. If you wish to borrow money or gain investors, you will need records to satisfy the bank and put together a prospectus. Potential purchasers of your business will also want to review your financial records. Last but not least, one of the most important reasons to keep proper records is that they makes it easy to prepare a tax return.

The actual books used to record business transactions are called **ledgers**. The pages in ledgers are divided into columns and rows. Entries are made onto a ledger page according to whether they are credits or debits - that is money paid to your business or money paid out. Many small business owners are too busy to do regular entries into ledgers so their receipts and expenses are kept in an orderly fashion - something better than a shoe box - for later recording. This is particularly true if the business receives payment at irregular periods. If you find yourself in this situation, try to complete the ledger entries once a month or so.

BOOKKEEPERS AND ACCOUNTANTS

The work involved in the orderly entry of business transactions is disagreeable to many people, but it is a profession to a **bookkeeper**. Small businesses usually do not require a full-time bookkeeper, but it is common for small businesses to have a part-time bookkeeper who spends a couple of hours a week or a month maintaining the books. The bookkeeper will spell out the kind of information required from you to maintain your books. This usually includes deposit books, ledgers, sales receipts and cash reports.

It is advisable to choose a bookkeeper who is familiar with your kind of business. It is also a good idea to get references from other businesses who have used the person you intend to retain. Both your expectations and those of the bookkeeper should be spelled out as you negotiate the fees for service. You might want a bookkeeper to take over any number of these business financial details: payroll preparation, general ledger entries, accounts payable and accounts receivable, income tax preparation, sales tax and GST submission.

Of course, there are also some excellent software programs available that are designed to maintain accounting books. These still require your time to set up accounts, input data and print out reports, but they do a much neater job than was possible with the old ledger book.

At year end, the books prepared and maintained by you or your bookkeeper can be passed on to an accountant. Although some bookkeepers prepare tax returns, it is advisable to retain the services of an accountant who has a professional accounting designation such as CA (Chartered Accountant) CMA (Certified Management Accountant) or CGA (Certified General Accountant).

Income tax preparation is a once-a-year task and the cost of using an accountant is minimal compared to the peace of mind it provides. The better your own record keeping is, the lower the fees of a accountant will be. The worst case scenario, one that is often related in a humorous way by bookkeepers and accountants, is the small business owner who arrives one day before the deadline for income tax submission with a shoe box full of receipts. This can be an expensive experience.

In addition to tax preparation, accountants are also a valuable resource when applying loans or discussing business matters with potential investors. If you choose not to retain a bookkeeper or accountant, there are many excellent books available on this subject, or you may wish to take a basic course in bookkeeping.

BUSINESS ACCOUNTING TERMS

The use of accountants and bookkeepers is a great way for small business owners to concentrate on the core aspects of their business. It is still important, however, for anyone in business to understand the terms and concepts involved in accounting. Knowledge of these terms and concepts will also allow small business owners to provide good information to their bookkeepers and accountants.

One good piece of advice for small business owners is to do your own books for at least a few months to get a "feel" for the accounting that's involved. While accounting and bookkeeping may not be a very exciting part of starting a new business, they are essential for a business to thrive. Understanding of the following terms will help:

Accounts payable Money that your business has to pay out - these are expenses that a business incurs; for example: office expenses, rent, materials, advertising, shipping, etc.

Accounts receivable Money that is owing to your business by customers or others. Accounts receivable are a valuable asset and may be sold or used as collateral for a loan. There are also businesses that specialize in buying accounts receivable from other businesses at a discount. They then collect payment from your customers, but you have received your cash right away.

Accruals There are two accounting systems for entering amounts in ledgers - the cash system and the accrual system. The cash system allows for the entry of receivable and payable amounts only when they are actually received or paid out. The accrual system requires those amounts to be entered when the invoices are sent out or received. Revenue Canada requires all businesses (except farmers) to use the accrual method of accounting. This means that you may have to include amounts as income that you actually haven't received yet.

Assets Any goods or property owned by a business are assets. These include equipment, real estate, vehicles, investments and even "good will."

Bill of sale and **receipt** A receipt book is a book of sequentially numbered sales receipts. These receipts are handwritten. There are two copies of each receipt, the original for the customer and a carbon copy for the business. At the end of the business day, a cash report and deposit can be prepared from these receipts.

A cash register produces a taped record of transactions. When a sale is rung in, the register may produce a printed receipt which is given to the customer in place of a handwritten sales receipt, although some businesses give both a cash register receipt and a handwritten sales receipt. All sales, refunds and voids are recorded on the tape. At the end of the day a cash report is prepared to balance the amounts on the tape with the cash, cheques and credit card slips in the register.

Book value The original cost of an asset minus the accumulated depreciation. Note that book value does not reflect the market value, the replacement cost or the liquidation value of an asset.

Capital The owner of a business usually invests assets at the start-up. This investment may consist of cash and other assets such as equipment. The total amount of the combined invested assets is called capital.

Cash This includes cheques, currency, money orders, bank drafts, credit card slips. See "accrual" for the cash system of accounting.

Cash flow When a small business begins operating the primary financial issue is the inflow or outflow of money. Inflow and outflow is called income and expenses. The flow of money into and out of accounts is called cash flow. Cash flow in small businesses can be divided into two kinds of income, daily and periodical. The income in businesses such as restaurants and retail stores is usually received daily. The income from service businesses may be billed monthly and therefore received monthly or bi-monthly.

Cash report Businesses such as retail stores or restaurants need a way to confirm on a daily basis how much money they will be depositing and that the amount is correct. An excellent way to do this is to have a daily cash report. A cash report is prepared at the end of the business day. It lists cash, cheques, credit card slips received and credit and refunds given. The amount of each item on the cash report is checked against a cash register tape or a stack of copies of sales receipts. Ideally the daily deposit balances with the tape or sales receipts. If a cash report does not balance it signals that there may be problems in the handling of cash in your business. This may mean carelessness or dishonesty by employees. In either case a review of procedures is necessary.

Collateral Assets pledged as security for a debt. Even small corporations usually require the owners to put up collateral to arrange for bank financing.

Costs Many business people do not have a good grasp of costs for a product or service. If you manufacture an item you need to know exactly how much it costs to produce it. Costing affects pricing. Obviously if the price of an product is less than the cost to produce it, the net result is a loss. Other costs which must be calculated in the price of each product or service include administrative costs. Costs not directly related to the product or service are called indirect costs.

Current account A chequing account used by businesses. When a business opens this type of account it receives a large-format cheque book and a large-format deposit book.

Depreciation The progressive devaluation of assets is a cost of doing business. Individuals experience the same thing when they purchase a vehicle. Compare the cost of a new car to its value when it is four years old. For tax purposes, a certain proportion of the value of a fixed asset can be written off each year as an expense. Revenue Canada provides a chart of rates of depreciation for this purpose.

Dividend An amount paid to a firm's ownership out of net income.

Equipment This includes any article expected to last for a period of years that necessary to conduct a business. Some kinds of equipment might include office furniture, tools, machines, store fixtures and vehicles. Equipment is depreciated for accounting and income tax purposes.

Inventory Stock on hand. In a manufacturing business inventory is the amount of unshipped completed product and the materials on hand to produce new product. In a retail business inventory is the total value of the goods in the store. "**Turns**" of inventory refer to how many times the entire stock may be replaced within a year. A store that holds $100,000 of inventory and does $500,000 of business a year has five "turns."

Invoice A bill sent to a customer after goods or services have been delivered.

Liabilities Money owed by a business; these may be short-term (a supplier who will wait 45 days for payment) or long-term (a mortgage or line-of-credit).

Mark-up An amount added to the cost of an item to arrive at the final selling price. Mark-ups can range from 3 percent at a supermarket to almost 1000 percent in cosmetics.

Merchandise is goods produced for sale or bought for resale at a profit.

Overdraft An agreement between a bank and a customer that cheques will be honored even if there is a shortage of funds in the account. Interest is charged on an overdraft balance, often at a higher rate than for a loan or line-of-credit.

Overhead The regular cost of operating your business. This may include: rent or lease payments, phones, utilities, office equipment, advertising and vehicles.

Payroll Wages paid to employees and contributions made to the government on their behalf.

Petty cash A small amount of money usually kept in a metal box which is used for miscellaneous items. When money is removed from petty cash a receipt is placed in the box. If a receipt is not available a note indicating who took the money and for what purpose should be provided. Petty cash is balanced monthly and a cheque written on the current account to replenish the amount expended. One caution about petty cash - if money is taken from petty cash and no receipt or note provided, it is impossible to balance the account.

Prepaid expenses are also an asset. These are expenses that are paid for prior to their use, for example stationery which is paid for on or near delivery, but used up over a long period of time.

Profit is the amount of cash left over after everything and everybody else is paid, including yourself.

Profit and loss (P&L) The balance between revenue and expenses is called profit and/or loss. Your estimated profit or loss should be recorded on a profit and loss projection report. Your actual profit or loss is recorded on a profit and loss statement. Both of these are best prepared in conjunction with an accountant.

Retained earnings Profit that is kept in reserve in the companies accounts. Retained earnings can act as a financial buffer if times get tough. Corporations can retain earning without being taxed on them immediately; sole proprietors and partnerships are taxed on earnings whether they are retained or paid out to the owners.

Statement A statement of account sent to a customer on a regular basis, either monthly or quarterly, which identifies all transactions in the period. A statement of account will show invoices and payments.

"**Terms**" (Actually terms of payment on accounts receivable.) If a customer is not paying cash on delivery, it must be understood when the bill will be paid. This may range from 10 days to 30 days. Terms of payment are usually spelled out on an invoice.

Working capital is cash on hand available for the daily operation of a business.

Am I making money yet?

The more complex the business, the more difficult it may be to figure out if you're really making money. One basic rule is "pay yourself first." As owner-manager, your salary should be drawn from the business on a regular basis. You must also figure long-term expenses - depreciation, equipment replacement, cash reserves, etc. - into the account books before you can calculate whether or not there is a profit. Then, and only then, can you award yourself a share of the profits. (And remember, there will be tax to pay on any profits you take out.)

CHAPTER SIX

Finding cash for your business

It is said that a majority of new business failures occur because most new ventures do not have sufficient financing to bring their products or services successfully to the market. Another adage is that a small businessperson should take whatever dollar figure you anticipate will be required for start-up and immediately add 50 percent. The break-even point is always higher and further away than you expect.

So where can money be found for start-up - and found again when working capital is growing tight? The answers vary depending on your personal circumstances.

Yourself It's never wise to begin a company by mortgaging your house, running up five credit cards to their limits and cashing in your RRSPs. But these things have all been done to keep companies afloat when prospects were solid but cash was running thin. Invariably, other lenders expect you to show your own faith in your company with a substantial investment of your own savings. If you're smart, you'll limit your investment to savings, period.

Friends and family Borrowing from friends and family to start a new business is not a good idea because, if your business fails, it is awfully difficult to notify those close to you that they have lost the money they lent to you. On the other hand, there is often no other source for start-up financing for young entrepreneurs. Friends and family know you, and perhaps believe in your abilities. They might be persuaded to invest start-up cash for a small partnership share in your company. If so, they should be approached with the same careful planning and formal application that you would use in approaching a bank.

Line-of-credit A line-of-credit is a set amount of credit available from a bank for an individual or business. Some small business owners use their personal line-of-credit to operate their businesses. A line-of-credit may be secured or non-secured, but banks ordinarily require any substantial line-of-credit to be secured. This usually means that you may be required to use the equity in your house as collateral for a line-of-credit. This is a move that begs the question "Do you really want to bet your house on the success of your business?"

A bank loan For larger loan amounts you may apply to a bank for a loan. Loans for specific items, such as equipment, are relatively easy to obtain because the item provides some of the required collateral. Loans for more general purposes such as operating capital are more difficult to obtain and financial institutions may require a business owner to have an equal amount of capital invested in the business. If the value of assets in the business such as receivables, inventory or real estate are not enough to cover the required collateral, you may be asked to assign personal assets such as stocks or the equity in your home. Once again this arrangement raises the possibility of losing your home if your business fails.

Banking is divided into consumer and commercial services. Consumer banking deals with the average customer who deposits personal money such as paycheques and takes personal loans for vehicles and such. Commercial banking offers services to business such as payroll accounts. A person starting a small business may be fortunate enough to bank with a branch that offers both consumer and commercial services, and therefore be able to use an existing banking relationship to start a commercial account. If the branch where you bank is a relatively small branch, the loans officer and bank manager may have limitations on amounts they are able to approve without the approval of a person higher in the organization. If your business is going to generate large volumes of cash flow and you need large lines-of-credit and/or loans, you might be better served if you start with a branch that specializes in commercial services. Once a bank is involved in the financing of your business, they will require regular reports on the activities of your business; in a way banks become partners in your enterprise.

Banks are conservative by nature and often do not provide the kind of debt financing that small businesses require. The federal government has a variety of programs to insure bank loans to small businesses. These programs are more or less available depending on the political climate and where you happen to live. Your bank manager should be able to discuss the availability of government-insured loans.

Venture capital There are companies that specialize in higher-risk loans. Higher risk means a higher rate of return for these companies, and subsequently a higher cost to the small business owner. If you have a solid business idea backed by good market research - and can convince a venture capitalist of your own ability to succeed - you may be able to obtain a substantial portion of start-up costs. As with banks, venture capitalists require a solid presentation including a business plan with backup financial reports.

FINANCIAL REPORTS

There are three basic financial reports which will be most useful to you and to your bank if you apply for a loan or other financing: a balance sheet (also called a statement of assets and liabilities), an income statement and a cash flow statement.

Of course, the main task of anyone who is starting a small business is to get the business operating and start bringing in cash, not to become an accountant. The following examples of financial reports are included so that you may understand how and why they are put together. In addition to the three basic reports, a bank or financial institution may require a statement of personal net worth, so an example of that is included. An accountant is always much better qualified to produce these reports based on the figures you provide.

Some conventions of accounting to remember The zeros representing thousands of dollars (such as $10,000 or $7,000,000) are always separated by commas. A line beneath a column of figures means that the list of numbers above the line is totaled below the line. A negative number or a number to be subtracted from another is preceded by a minus sign "-" or enclosed in brackets ($2,000).

SAMPLE STATEMENT OF ASSETS AND LIABILITIES

ACME CHEESE CO., LTD.

STATEMENT OF ASSETS AND LIABILITIES

For the periods ending December 31, 2004 & 2005

ASSETS		
Current assets	**2004**	**2005**
Cash	$ 35,000	$ 17,500
Accounts receivable	$ 40,000	$ 92,500
Inventory	$ 75,000	$ 57,500
Total current assets	$ 150,000	$ 157,500
Fixed assets		
Land and buildings	$ 110,000	$ 110,000
Equipment	$ 78,750	$ 105,000
Less accumulated depreciation	$ (43,750)	$ (52,500)
Total fixed assets	$ 145,000	$ 162,500
TOTAL ASSETS	**$ 295,000**	**$ 300,000**
LIABILITIES AND EQUITY		
Current liabilities		
Accounts payable	$ 40,000	$ 92,500
Short-term loans (Notes)	$ 52,500	$ 70,000
Accrued expenses	$ 17,500	$ 17,500
Total current liabilities	$ 110,000	$ 180,000
Long-term liabilities		
Mortgages	$ 131,250	$ 122,500
TOTAL LIABILITIES	**$ 241,250**	**$ 302,500**
EQUITY		
Net equity (Owners stock)	$ 87,500	$ 87,500
Retained earnings	$ 166,250	$ 210,000
Total equity	**$ 253,750**	**$ 297,500**
Total liabilities and equity	**$ 495,000**	**$ 600,000**

The balance sheet should be prepared by an accountant. The first section of the statement lists the value of the resources available and owned by the business. There are two categories of assets: current assets and fixed assets.

Current assets are receivables, cash on hand and inventory. These are items that, if not already in cash form, are expected to be converted into cash within the normal cycle of business. For example, an account receivable is expected to be paid within the terms of payment, usually 30, 60 or 90 days. Assets that can be turned easily into cash are said to be "liquid." For accounting purposes assets that can be made liquid within one year are identified as current assets.

Fixed assets are equipment, land, buildings and vehicles. By nature these are long-term, permanent items. These items are purchased for the operation of the business and as such will not be converted into cash. They also usually reduce in value over time (depreciation), therefore this amount is deducted to show their real value.

Long-term investments are assets such as loans or notes owed to the business which will be repaid over a long period of time.

The list of liabilities shows the source of the funds that produced the assets. The current liabilities are amounts that would normally be paid within one year. Long-term liabilities are amounts that are expected to be paid over a number of years, such as a mortgage.

Owners' equity is the amount the owners actually invested in the business.

Retained earnings are amounts that have not been withdrawn or paid to the owners as dividends. Acme Cheese is incorporated, so its earning can be retained.

Note that the total assets must always equal the total liabilities. That's why this is called a "balance sheet."

ACME CHEESE CO., LTD.

ANNUAL INCOME STATEMENT

December 31, 2004 to December 31, 2005

		% of 2004 Sales		% of 2005 Sales
Net sales	$ 770,000	100.0%	$ 875,000	100.0%
Cost of sales	$ 481,250	61.9%	$ 525,000	60.0%
Gross profit	$ 288,750	38.1%	$ 350,000	40.0%
Operating expenses:				
Salaries	$ 110,250	14.2	$ 120,750	13.8
Payroll expenses	$ 12,250	1.6	$ 14,000	1.6
Utilities	$ 7,000	0.9	$ 8,750	1.6
Insurance	$ 15,750	2.0	$ 15,750	1.8
Advertising	$ 8,750	1.1	$ 8,750	1.0
Maintenance	$ 10,500	1.4	$ 10,500	1.2
Supplies	$ 7,000	0.9	$ 7,000	0.8
Accounting	$ 5,250	0.7	$ 5,250	0.6
Depreciation	$ 8,750	1.1	$ 8,750	1.0
Total operating expense	$ 185,500	25.7%	$ 199,500	24.4%
Net operating income	$ 103,250	12.4%	$ 136,500	15.3%
Less interest expense	$ (5,250)	0.7	$ (3,500)	1.3
Net taxable income	$ 91,000	11.7%	$ 140,000	14.0%
Less income tax	$ 31,500	4.0	$ 45,500	4.2
Net income	$ 59,500	7.7%	$ 87,500	9.8%

Schedule of retained earnings 2005

Retained earnings from 2004	$166,250
Net income 2005	$ 87,500
Minus dividends paid	$(43,750)
Retained earnings 2005	$210,000

The Income Statement is a report of the revenue within a given period of time and the expenses that were incurred in producing that revenue. Each item is expressed as an amount and as a percentage of the net sales.

Two years are reported so that variance in amounts, percentages and ratios may be noted.

Net sales is the total income derived by Acme Cheese selling its product to customers. Anyone perusing this statement would immediately notice that Acme had a 10 percent increase in net sales.

Cost of sales is the amount expended directly to produce the product, in this case, cheese. Some expenses included in this figure would be the cost of milk, additives and the equipment to make the cheese. These are called direct costs. Business people like to know how much it is costing to produce an item or unit of product so that they can mark it up properly. From the percent column you can see that Acme decreased the cost of production by 0.4 percent.

Gross profit is the difference between the net sales and the cost of sales. Since Acme Cheese had higher net sales and lower cost of sales, the gross profit has gone up from 2004 to 2005.

Other costs of doing business, not directly related to the production of an item or the rendering of a service, are called **indirect costs** or **operating expenses**. These include overhead expenses such as salaries and insurance which are ongoing and unchanged by the level of production. Although there were variances in each item of operating expenses for the two years, the overall percentage related to net sales is lower. Therefore, although Acme spent more money on operating expenses, they are ahead of the game.

Total operating expenses are subtracted from the gross profit to produce the net operating income. This amount is further reduced by the cost of the interest for any loans a company may have, in this case $100,000.

The resulting amount is called **net taxable income** on which the amount of payable tax is calculated, in Acme's case 30 percent.

The final amount arrived at after all deductions is called **net income**.

If a company produces more net income than is required to pay dividends, some income may be retained by the company. These are called retained earnings and may be held as investment certificates or bonds which in turn will produce interest income for the company. These amounts are useful to companies when financing is required for growth or to provide operating capital during tough times.

ACME CHEESE CO., LTD.

CASH FLOW STATEMENT

For the period ending December 31, 2005

Cash flow from operations (CFFO)	
Net income	$ 87,500
Plus depreciation	$ 8,750
Minus increase in accounts receivables	$ (52,500)
Minus increase in inventory	$ (52,500)
Plus increase in accounts payable	$ 52,500
Plus changes in accrued expenses	$ 0
Cash flow from operations	$ 43,750
Cash flow from investing activities	
Minus increase in fixed assets	$ (26,250)
Cash flow from investing activities	$ (26,250)
Cash flow from financing activities	
Plus increase in short-term loans	$ 17,500
Minus decrease in mortgage payable	$ (8,750)
Minus dividends paid	$ (43,750)
Cash flow from financing activities	$ (35,000)
Net cash flow	**$ (17,500)**
Reconciliation	
Change in cash account 2004 to 2005	$ (17,500)
Net cash flow	$ (17,500)
Difference	$ 0

The purpose of the cash flow statement is to measure the cash from operations rather than profit from operations. Even a profitable company needs cash flow to finance normal operations, invest in new assets and provide the cash to service new debt. There are three parts to the cash flow statement: the cash flow from operations, the cash flow from investing activities, and the cash flow from financing Activities. Cash flows may be inflows or outflows, pluses or minuses.

Cash flow from operations (CFFO) - is the most important part of the cash flow statement because it indicates the inflow of cash, which in turn determines the ability to operate. The first amount, **net income**, is derived from the annual income statement. This amount is adjusted to reflect a true picture of cash inflow to the business by adding back in amounts that were deducted on the income statement but were not real cash items, such as the $8,750 depreciation amount. The rest of the calculations relate to items that either tie up or free up cash.

The first item after depreciation, **increase in accounts receivable**, is derived from the balance sheet. This is money that was not collected and represents a drain on Acme's CFFO. Increase in inventory ties up cash and is also a drain on Acme's CFFO and is therefore a minus factor. **Increase in accounts payable** is a positive factor in the calculation because it represents cash not paid out. **Accrued expenses** is a positive factor because this amount represents expenses that have been incurred but not paid for, therefore the cash for these items is still in Acme's hands.

Cash flow from investing activities (CFFIA) and **cash flow from financing activities (CFFFA)** represent changes in the companies non-operating cash activities. In Acme's case changes occurred in fixed assets, notes payable, long-term liabilities and equity items. Acme's increase in fixed assets resulted in an investment in additional fixed assets. Something must have been purchased leading to an outflow of cash.

The financing section indicates that Acme raised $17,500 in short-term financing, but this was offset when long-term debt was reduced by $8,750 and dividends of $43,750 were paid out. The net result of financing activities is therefore a $35,000 outflow.

Net cash flow is the balance when CFFIA and CFFIA is deducted from CFFO.

PERSONAL FINANCIAL STATEMENT

Name:____

Address:______________________________________

____________________ Telephone:__________________

ASSETS	
Cash	$ 2,000
Bank accounts	$ 5,000
Real estate	$120,000
Registered Retirement Plans	$ 60,000
Stocks	$ 10,000
Vehicles	$ 15,000
Accounts receivable	$ 12,000
Chattels and other liquid assets (boats, coin collections etc.)	$ 5,000
TOTAL ASSETS	$290,000
LIABILITIES	
Mortgages	$100,000
Credit card balances	$ 2,000
Bank loans	$ 5,000
Accounts payable	$ 6,000
Outstanding taxes	$ 2,500
TOTAL LIABILITIES	$115,500
NET WORTH (assets minus liabilities)	$174,500

The personal net worth statement is very similar to the statement of assets and liabilities for a business. Most banks produce a statement of net worth for personal loan applicants for their own files. You or your accountant should produce your own before you meet with your banker or other financier. It shows you are organized and aware. You will also have more control over its content.

BUSINESS PLANS

Most lenders and potential investors in a new enterprise will expect that your ideas and plans have been set down in a written format: a business plan. This plan can provide a framework of reference for growth, and adds to your chances of business success. It is a good idea to update your business plan on a yearly basis.

Three reasons for writing up a business plan:

- it gives you the opportunity to think through what you want to accomplish and how you are going to accomplish it
- it shows investors or backers that you are organized and business-like; in fact, it forces you to get your plans and financials in order
- banks and other institutions require it for financing

There is no set format for a business plan. The basic ideas should be on the first page, subsequent details of the enterprise, product, service and financial set-up should follow on the next few pages. No one is particularly impressed by a 100-page business plan (nor are they likely to read it), but enough detail must be provided to show that you have thought through the issues in starting your company.

There are software programs which will take you, step-by-step, through the writing of a business plan. Often these are helpful in pinpointing the issues you need to address. On the other hand, no generic program can lay out the perfect plan for your business and your situation.

The following sample is a short version of a complete business plan for the fictitious cheese producer Acme Cheese Company, Ltd. Each section could be added to and revised to suit a different type and size of business.

BUSINESS PLAN FOR ACME CHEESE COMPANY, LTD.

History

Acme Cheese Company, Ltd. is a producer of a variety of fine cheeses. It was started as a part-time enterprise by John Gouda on the family farm in 1978. At first, the cheese was made and sold in the farm's dairy. In 1982 John's wife, Mary, started selling the cheese at a booth at the local farmer's market. Soon they were supplying local stores and two years later the dairy was expanded and John signed his first order to supply an upscale chain of food stores with a variety of specialty cheeses. By 1999 a retail store was added to the dairy and the wholesale business stretched across Canada. The company is registered as a limited corporation, 75 percent of the stock is held by the Gouda family and 25 percent by employees.

Product

High quality specialty cheeses with distinctive flavors.

Market

The retail customers are affluent, middle-aged people who spend a portion of their disposable income on gourmet food products. The trend towards high-end food products by the baby boomer generation is well documented. These are the primary customers.

Pricing - High-end price point

Terms - Retail is over-the-counter cash, wholesale is 30 days with 2 percent discount for payment within ten days

Competition - None locally, nationally Acme competes against the better producers of specialty cheeses as well as imported cheese from Europe.

Management

Key personnel (resumes attached)

J.T. Gouda	- president
T. Peccorino	- vice president finance C.A.
Cam Embert	- personnel manager
Harry Smally	- plant manager
Maria Ricotta	- credit manager
Nigel Berriman	- farm manager

Farm, dairy and plant

Two hundred acres of prime farmland with a herd of prize-winning dairy cattle.

Equipment - state-of-the-art milk handling and cheese making equipment.

Vehicles - five milk trucks, two pickup trucks, 1 4X4 with snow plow.

Office - Adjacent to the plant - fully computerized accounting.

Employees - Twenty.

Inventory - $100,000 of cheese produced per week.

Scheduling - Highest volume is produced in the fall and winter. There is an increase in sales from the retail operation during the summer months.

Financing

Statement of income	(Attached)
Statement of assets and liabilities	(Attached)
Cash flow statement	(Attached)
Projection	$4,000,000 per year by 2004

Supporting consultants

Bank - Bank of Canada

Lawyer - Susan Bonhomme - Spring, Wing and Bonhomme

Accountant - Susan Quark

Of course, each item in this business plan could be expanded to produce a sizeable document. For a small venture, a business plan of four to five pages with backup documents would be sufficient.

FINANCIAL PROJECTIONS

Part of planning business operations is making an estimate of costs, business volume and profit. If you are just starting out, you will have to project all of the numbers for the new venture. This first year of operation is the most difficult to project. Subsequent years become easier when a history has been established. Most businesses plan for a modest growth per year based on market conditions, economic factors and their own ability to handle more business. Once you have been in business for a few years, you can use the annual income statements for comparisons.

CHAPTER SEVEN

Marketing your product or service

The first axiom of marketing is "know thy customer." One way to do this is to make use of the information found in demographic studies produced by Statistics Canada or commercial marketing firms. This data can be used to figure out how many of your potential customers are in a particular age range, how much money they make, how much disposable income they have, where they live and so on. All this information can be valuable to you in estimating the future success of your particular product or service.

A group much discussed by demographers is the baby boom generation born after World War II, roughly between 1946 and 1965. More babies were born in this period than at any other comparable period in recent history. This baby-boom phenomenon has been a delight to social scientists, marketers and authors ever since. Since there have been more baby boom customers of a certain age at a certain time period, governments and businesses could tailor their operations to satisfy the needs of this group. To illustrate, consider that the oldest baby boomers in 1998 were fifty years old. As an aging population they require increasing amounts of medical care. A smart entrepreneur can anticipate a future boom in seniors-oriented recreational facilities and travel packages, and then in retirement and nursing homes. After the year 2017 there will likely be a boom in funeral services and cemetery plots related to this group.

Baby boomers are such a large group that demographers have divided them up into sub-groups. One group that receives a lot of press is Generation X. This group is made up of tail-end baby boomers. The most remarkable feature of Generation Xers is their desire to stand out from the older baby boomers. The popularity of extreme sports by Generation Xers is a good example. Marketers have picked up on this trend and have directed advertising and promotions accordingly.

The **market** is the entire population of consumers.

Marketing is the process of figuring out what products or services will be bought by which customers and when.

Marketer is a business person who endeavors to optimize the match between product and customer.

Mass marketing means a single marketing strategy is used to offer the same product to all consumers.

Case study is the study of a real or hypothetical business situation from which a valuable lesson in business management may be learned.

Demographics is the study of population and is used by business to identify distinctive groups of consumers within the larger population.

Positioning is marketing so that a certain market segment will respond to your product or advertising.

Price point is the point at which a customer begins to balk at a purchase.

Segmentation means classifying the market into sub-groups which share similar features.

Target means directing advertising and promotions at a certain market segment that seems more rewarding than others.

Trend is an increase in a specific consumer preference within the market.

Of course, demographics are only one part of the larger marketing picture. Other marketing considerations are less global but will definitely impact on your business. A smart businessperson asks and answers a number of strategic marketing questions before setting up shop or hanging out a shingle.

- How many competitors do you face?
- How does your product or service compare to that offered by your competitors?
- Is the market for your product or service increasing or decreasing?
- What are the economic and population trends for your immediate area?
- What are the characteristics of your target customer?
- What form of advertising will be most effective for this group?

Extensive market research is expensive and time-consuming. Although you may not be in a position to expend the time, energy and money to do intensive market research when you are starting your business, it is advisable to do as much as you can. Some businesses fail because they did not pay attention to market factors. The following history will illustrate this point. The case study is not fiction, but the names and details have been changed in our presentation.

A CASE STUDY: FIVE RESTAURANTS

The restaurant/bar is a roadside establishment common throughout North America. This one, originally called "Family Restaurant," is located in the countryside on a two-lane, semi-major highway that was the major local thoroughfare before a four-lane super highway was built a few kilometres away. Initially, the restaurant flourished from drive-by business. It served family-style food at a good price; alcohol was served as an incidental item. After the new highway was built, business steadily dropped off and the owners decided to sell the restaurant and retire.

"Joel" bought the business in the 1983. He had many years of experience in the restaurant and bar business and was ready to start his own enterprise. In recent years, Joel had noticed an increase in the number of young people in their twenties going out to bars. He realized that there were no bars catering to this market within ten miles of the old "Family Restaurant." Joel figured he could provide cheap beer, live entertainment and grilled food to this growing market of young consumers, so he re-opened the restaurant as "Joe Cool's Place." His estimates were right: he ran the restaurant for ten years and made a pile of money.

In the early 1990s, Joel noticed a decrease in customer volume. The nearby baby boomers were getting married and raising families. He decided to sell his restaurant and buy a business which serviced home computers. His new business was called "Crazy Joel's," and it, too, did quite well.

The purchaser's of Joel's old restaurant, Susan and David had ideas of their own. They were great cooks and wanted a restaurant with a theme. The theme was taken from a book and movie which had been popular a year earlier. They used their savings and a loan from their families to renovate Joe Cool's Place to reflect the new theme, "Space Adventure." They advertised in the local papers and due to the novelty of the theme and the quality of the food they did well for a couple of years. When the novelty wore off and the locals realized they were paying a premium for what otherwise is called a hamburger, business dropped dramatically. Faced with impending bankruptcy, Susan and David bailed out and sold the business to Harry.

Harry had a good job at a nearby electronics plant, his house was paid for and he had quite a bit of money saved up. Harry's wife, Stella, made the best Bokkernonian stew in the world and Harry figured all she needed was a restaurant and the world would beat a path to her door. Unfortunately, there weren't very many Bokkernonians living near the restaurant and the price of Harry's beer was higher than that at any local bar. Stella's stew was tasty but permeated the restaurant with an odor most people were unfamiliar with. Harry's "Bokkernonian Restaurant" lasted 18 months, but he lost his savings before he could sell the restaurant.

Naomi, who had been driving by the restaurant for many years on her way to her cottage, had been watching the various transmutations of the restaurant. Naomi had owned and operated various successful businesses and was a sharp marketer. She quickly realized that Harry's "Bokkernonian Restaurant" wasn't going to make it and had done some market research of her own. She bought a demographic study that had been done on the area surrounding the restaurant. The results of this study showed that the local population was affluent, middle-aged and there were a lot of horse farms in the area. There were no restaurants catering to the horsey set within fifteen miles. She also knew from personal experience that there was a great many cottagers driving by the restaurant throughout the summer.

When Harry went broke, Naomi was ready. She bought the property at a bargain price. She hired a designer to create an upscale English country inn motif, both interior and exterior, to suit the new name of "Carriage Club." The chef she hired created a menu to suit, and the staff was trained to give a high level of service. An extensive wine list was offered with prices to reflect the ambience and quality of food and service.

Naomi ran the restaurant for five years, breaking even in the first year and making a profit each year thereafter. As an entrepreneur, Naomi wanted to investigate other business opportunities, so she sold the restaurant for a profit and went on to other ventures.

There are some morals in this history:

- Joel succeeded because he saw a trend, knew how to cater to it and was in the right place at the right time.
- Susan and David failed because they relied on a fad.
- Harry failed because he didn't understand his customers.
- Naomi succeeded because she was a smart marketer and did her homework.

Doomed from the start

The worst reason to start a business is to help out a family member who is in trouble. The recipient of your charity won't appreciate it and won't really commit to the business; nor will you be prepared to make the sacrifices of time and money to make such an enterprise a success.

UNDERSTANDING YOUR CUSTOMER

Besides control over finances, no single factor is more important in business success than understanding the needs and wants of your customers. It is possible to hire marketing companies to find answers to these basic questions, but the cost for this can be substantial. A smart business person can do much of this, themselves, by considering the answers to 10 basic questions.

1. How old is the person who will likely buy my product?
2. Is that person male or female, married or single?
3. Will this person drive to my place of business or take public transport?
4. How much money is my customer likely to spend?
5. What kind of service will they expect?
6. How long will my customer expect the product to last?
7. Will my customer be motivated by a special offer?
8. How important is price point?
9. Do I expect my customer to come back?
10. Where does my customer live?

The importance of the answers to these questions will vary from one business to another. To illustrate the kind of answers you can expect to these questions, let's consider the customers of Acme Cheese Company, Limited, the fictitious producer, wholesaler and retailer of cheese whose financials we looked at in the last chapter. Almost everyone eats cheese, and rather than compete against the industrial producers of cheese, Acme directs their marketing towards a niche group of discerning consumers who buy specialty cheeses. There are two facets to Acme's business – wholesale and retail. The wholesale side of the business is directed at specialty cheese stores and to large grocery chains that have a gourmet or specialty food section in their stores. The retail side of the business began as a way of supplementing income on the family dairy farm. As the business grew the retail side became the primary source of income and the basis for future expansion of the business.

Now let's consider the 10 questions above in terms of Acme Cheese's marketing plan.

Question 1 - Children and teenagers who think Cheese Whiz is the king of foods do not buy specialty cheese, therefore the answer to question 1 is - adults. Because Acme sells pricey specialty cheeses, the adults are likely to be over 30 and reasonably affluent.

Question 2 - Gender and marital status are irrelevant, except that more couples may do elegant entertaining than singles and therefore be more likely to buy specialty cheeses.

Question 3 - The retail outlet of Acme Cheese is located just outside Blyth, Ontario, on a secondary highway and therefore there is no walk-in traffic. On the other hand, in addition to their regular rural customers, many city people on their way to cottages stop in to buy some cheese. Acme has gone out of their way to provide easy access from the highway, clear signs leading to the store and a large paved parking lot.

Question 4 - Many of Acme's customers stock up with cheese and the average sale is $50.00.

Question 5 - Acme's customers require personalized service. They may wish to taste a sample of the cheese and to discuss the contents and method of manufacture. They respond to attentive, polite, knowledgeable service.

Question 6 - Since Acme produces various types of cheese that have different storage and life spans, Acme personnel go out of their way to discuss the storage and use of their cheeses.

Question 7 - Acme markets a high quality product at a premium price. Sales or discounts might cheapen the perception of their product. However, as a reward to regular customers, Acme occasionally offers some of their most expensive cheeses at a discount.

Question 8 - Acme could not compete with bulk industrial producers of cheese, and therefore they market their offering based on quality and variety. Their customers are the same ones who will pay a premium for a fine bottle of wine and a variety of imported specialty foods. Price is not a major factor.

Question 9 - Most certainly, Acme's success is based on return business.

Question 10 - There are two categories of customers, locals and drive-by. Acme advertises in the local paper throughout the year. They also advertise in larger city newspapers during the summer to attract people going to their cottages.

Acme's dairy, cheese factory and store are neat, tidy and attractive. The exterior of the business has a rustic motif; the interior decor was done professionally. There is more than adequate parking space. The staff is trained to provide a high level of service. Whenever possible, the company president gives his personal attention to each customer. The Acme Cheese product is expensive, the quality, service and ambience support a high price and the customers can afford it; in fact the high price may be an incentive for them to buy. The company directs their advertising to upscale publications and a classical music program on FM radio. Constant sales promotions might cheapen the product, therefore Acme has only one annual sale and sends an invitation for that event to past customers.

All of this may seem quite straightforward when applied to *another* company's product or service, but it's often easy to avoid this kind of analysis of your own company's markets. Effective marketing may seem a simple mix of common sense, thoughtful analysis and sophisticated demographics, but it is as essential as financial planning to your company's success.

HOW AND WHERE TO SELL YOUR PRODUCT

Advertising is one of the best ways of spreading the word about your product or service. The three main media for advertising are print, radio and television. Print advertising includes newspapers, phone books, brochures, business cards, flyers and anything else that appears on paper. Let's consider each of these.

Newspaper advertising is often the least expensive form of mass advertising and is therefore the most popular with small business. Most newspapers will assist small business owners in the preparation of art work. Once business volume justifies it, you may wish to retain an advertising agency to prepare your material.

Your business **stationery** also advertises your name and product. This includes letterhead, envelopes, business cards, business forms and brochures. Extra time spent designing stationery will pay off later.

If you have a flair for design you may wish to try one of the desktop-publishing programs and create your own logo and letterhead. Many printing companies offer a design service to their customers. The cost of using a printer varies with the amount of artwork, the quality and volume of stationery you order. Another option is to use the printing service of an office supply store. The quality of the stationery they produce may not match that of a printing company, but the cost is quite low. All printers provide a selection of prepared designs to choose from.

In major urban centers, **flyers** are often considerably cheaper than newspaper advertising, especially if your market is based in the local neighborhood. Printers often have connections to distribution companies that will deliver cheaply door-to-door.

The telephone book **Yellow Pages** have been proven to provide a certain volume of business to those who use this form of advertising. Since the Yellow Pages are published once a year it takes a while to get your ad in the book. As well, some communities have a number of different Yellow Pages - city-wide, neighborhood, etc. - and the combined cost for all these can be quite hefty. Nonetheless, for those who offer a service such as plumbing or computer repair, Yellow Pages ads quickly pay for themselves.

Direct mail is a form of print advertising that includes flyers and catalogues. This is where it is important to know where your potential customer lives. There are companies who specialize in creating and delivering flyers and catalogues. You can create the artwork for your flyers with a desktop-publishing program or have a company do it for you. Canada Post offers a special rate for a "drop" in a set number of postal codes, though the actual delivery date of the material may vary by several weeks.

Radio advertising is expensive in large markets, but is often very affordable in small towns and rural areas. These smaller radio stations are keen to gain advertisers' business since, unlike newspapers, commercials are their only source of income. If you have the budget for radio advertising, the radio station will arrange for the production of your commercial, and advise on the best times to air it. An important concept for this medium is "saturation," the number of times your advertisement has to air before potential customers are likely to pay attention. While an individual 30-second commercial might sell for a few dollars in "C" time slots when few people are listening, a "saturation" campaign in AA or A time slots can easily cost thousands of dollars.

Television advertising is usually prohibitively expensive for a small business. Sometimes distribution companies will prepare and place television ads if they can obtain your product at a sufficient discount, but most television commercials cost thousands if not hundreds of thousands of dollars to produce, and each airing will be at least several hundred dollars. It's rare for a small business to be able to afford these costs.

The advantage of **mail order** is that the overhead of having a retail operation is unnecessary. Once orders have been received from customers from an advertisement or a catalogue, it is a matter of shipping the merchandise from a warehouse and processing payment. For some products, this is a very effective means for both advertising and sales.

The Internet It has been estimated that by the year 2010, up to half of all products sold will be sold over the Internet. The Internet has had a meteoric and rocky rise in popularity and those who deny its significance do so at their own peril. Access to products on the Internet is excellent and the security-of-payment problem has been solved. But selling merchandise over the Internet is really just another form of mail order - somehow your customer has to be made aware of your site.

One of the reasons that the Internet might become an effective place to market goods and services is the large geographic area that may be serviced at no extra cost. Imagine, if you set up a commercial site, your products and services may be viewed by anyone in the world who has access to the Internet.

Some of the most successful commercial Internet sites are brokers. These small businesspeople have no inventory of their own; they merely match products with customers. One successful Internet business provides a worldwide supply of computer parts such as memory chips. Manufactures of computers require these parts at different times, in different quantities and need different types. This particular business advertises the availability of these components. If a sale is made they arrange for shipment directly to the customer. The billing and payment are handled electronically. The broker never sees the product. Such a system could be used to sell products from fly fishing gear to books to vacuum tubes and a multitude of other products.

SALES AGENTS

Sales agents are business people who specialize in selling manufacturers' products to retailers. They may have a number of products from different companies, but usually these products are in the same category of merchandise. The total package of all the items sales agents handle is called their **line**. The geographic area they cover is called their **territory**. If you are a manufacturer of one or two items, it is not usually cost-effective to hire your own sales force. Sales agents are paid a commission on actual sales, therefore they are a great way for a small business to give a product maximum exposure at minimal cost. You can find an appropriate agent by networking or by checking with retailers who would handle your product.

RETAIL STORES

Regardless of the growing popularity of alternative forms of shopping, going to a store will always appeal to certain shoppers. Aside from the fact that some people would like to make retail shopping an Olympic sport, there are some very good reasons why people prefer shopping in a store:

- Going out to shop is a social event for many people.
- Going out to shop can be a recreational activity, especially if the trip is to an area of specialty stores.
- Some people enjoy the personal, face-to-face service they may receive from store owners.
- Some people need to touch or see merchandise before buying.
- The sales transaction is immediate. The customer pays for and takes away the merchandise at the same time.

Basic principles of retail

- The three most important factors: location, location and location.
- Make it easy for your customers to travel to your store. Locations on major public transportation routes are prime spots. If customers are going to drive to your store, make sure that there is adequate parking nearby.
- Select a location where you will benefit from a large flow of pedestrian traffic.
- Design the exterior of the store so that it encourages customers to enter.
- Use window displays to tell passers-by something about your store and merchandise.
- Keep the your store spotlessly clean and tidy. A messy store doesn't bring customers back.
- Make sure your staff are well-groomed and attired appropriately and that they are polite and courteous.
- Keep the store well lit. A dingy store isn't cheerful.
- A well-stocked store looks prosperous and encourages sales.
- Quiet background music is a good way to add to the ambience of a store.

It is amazing how many retail operations will handle all of the basics well and yet fail in the most important point of all - making the transfer of merchandise for cash. It is unconscionable for staff to have a private conversation in front a customer who is waiting to pay. It is poor planning to have customers wait in line an inordinate amount of time to pay for a purchase. Retailers wait for peak sales time to make their profit - why have customers walk out because they get tired of waiting to pay? A smart retailer schedules extra staff at the cash at peak hours and over the holiday season.

When it gets really busy get an extra cash register and have personnel designated to ring in sales and other staff to pack it. One industry that really has this down to a fine art is the large chain grocery stores. Retailers can hire consultants to outline the plusses and minuses of their operation, but sometimes a watchful friend and two open eyes can give very similar information on how to improve customer service.

If you manufacturer a product, you may wish to sell it directly to the public through your own retail store. If the store is connected directly to a factory, it is sometimes called a "factory outlet." The suggestion is that the product can be bought at a greater discount than if it were sold at a regular store. Of course, the suggestion is mostly false - otherwise regular retailers would be up in arms. A factory outlet mostly serves to dispose of unsuccessful products, store returns and other items.

TELEMARKETING

The telephone is a powerful tool for selling products and services. We have all received annoying calls from someone trying to sell us something that we don't want. Although most calls made by telemarketers are unproductive, a certain percentage will be fruitful. Therefore the secret of successful telemarketing is the same as success in fishing. Professional tournament participants make thousands more casts than the average fisherman. Their success is not luck or skill, it's plain hard work. The same applies to telemarketing - the more calls, the more sales. There are companies that specialize in telemarketing and will contract for a commission to sell your product.

CHAPTER EIGHT

How to get organized

Disorganization is a great disadvantage when operating a small business. The converse, being organized, saves time and money and is a way of staying on top of your affairs. As the top person in your organization, it is up to you to impose order on your business activities. There are generally three areas in business that can benefit from being organized: your personal time, storage and retrieval of information and operating systems.

> "Time is money … bill for it!"

ORGANIZING TIME

Day planners or daily diaries are a great way to keep track of appointments, addresses and phone numbers. The best ones have at least one page for each day, (don't buy the really large ones, they are inconvenient for carrying around). Some journals or diaries also have a separate daily page for a "to do" list.

Daily diaries are also excellent for keeping track of travel and entertainment expenses. If you get audited, Revenue Canada may wish to look at your diary, therefore be diligent about the entries you make since they may save you money. When you start a new diary at the beginning of the year, transfer over all important addresses and phone numbers and store the old diary for future reference.

Address files (also known as business card files, Rolodex, or contact list database files.) You will probably accumulate a large number of addresses and phone numbers that are important to the operation of your business. There are various ways you can store these valuable pieces of information. You may prefer a desktop rotary file which uses a drum mechanism loaded with cards on which you can write addresses and phone numbers. Some of these rotary files have a way of inserting business cards which saves the trouble of writing the information down. Another convenient way of storing business cards is in books which have plastic pages with divisions for inserting business cards. Alternately you can staple a business card to a file folder which contains other relevant information.

There are also hand-held electronic organizers that allow for the entry and deletion of addresses and phone numbers. These are handy for anyone who works on the road. Many business people now use computer database programs in which they may store addresses and phone numbers. Some of these programs can dial a number automatically or insert an address in a word-processed letter.

To do lists Many successful business people take a few minutes at the beginning of their business day to sit down and itemize every task they want to get done that day. A regular, lined notepad is fine for this list. Include everything you want to accomplish on a given day, even your personal items. Give each task a number. As each task is completed, cross it out. If you don't complete a certain item add it to the next day's list.

Desktop planners If you spend a large part of your day at a desk, a desk planner is a great way to jot down phone numbers, appointments or information you are receiving from someone you are speaking to on the phone. These items should be transferred to your diary later for a permanent record. The main advantage of a desktop planner is that is right in front of you. It's a lot easier to remember something when its staring you in the face, as opposed to being hidden in a file or diary.

Chalkboards, vinyl boards, Post-its All of these are sensible ways to keep important items or issues front and centre. When you post items on a board, it also facilitates discussions with other people or groups. It also makes longer-term planning, vacation scheduling and appointment-keeping that much easier.

Tape-recorders and cameras Tape-recorders and cameras are great memory aids and can relieve you of tedious note taking. Micro tape-recorders that can be held in the palm of the hand are convenient for recording ideas, thoughts, reminders. These can be played back later and important items written down. Likewise cameras, both video and still, are handy devices for creating a permanent record of conditions, people, products or events. Some companies now photograph samples when placing an order so that they can compare the delivered goods with the order.

Meetings Meetings are an efficient way to bring people together to discuss a common issue in business. Unfortunately many business meetings are unorganized and unproductive; they become a waste of time and therefore a waste of money. The suggestions below will allow you to organize and run an effective business meeting.

- Ask the people you wish to attend for a suitable date and time for the meeting.
- Once a consensus has been reached on the timing, send out a notice at least one day ahead to remind people.
- Include an agenda or topic with the notice.
- When the meeting starts, a person should be identified as chairperson. It is this person's job to keep the meeting orderly and on track. The chairperson or another member may record the proceedings.

The written proceedings of a meeting are called the "minutes." Each topic should be raised separately and each person should have the chance to include his or her input on the issue. It is a good idea to start at one side of the table and go around until everyone has been included in the discussion. There should be an "action" column on the right hand side of each item indicating who is responsible for the resolution of that item. (Of course, an item may sometimes be inserted for informational purposes only, so no action is required.) The minutes should be given or mailed to the attendees and anyone else to whom the minutes may have significance. If a subsequent meeting is held on the same issues, call the attendees who were noted under the action column to ask them how their work is going.

Person-to-person meetings do not require such a formal format. It is still necessary for the two parties to set a time and place and expect each other to be there. (Nothing is more annoying to business people than to have time set aside for a meeting and the other party doesn't show up.) Rather than setting up a formal agenda or taking minutes, simply think through the issues that need discussion and take a few notes in your daily diary as the meeting proceeds. Follow-through is very important for these small meetings: always do exactly what you promised to do, or you may lose a customer or a client.

Some advice on meetings

- Avoid being called into a meeting on the spur of the moment.
- Never attend a meeting where you don't know the agenda.
- Review the minutes of the previous meeting before you sit down at the next one.
- If someone springs a surprise on you during any meeting, give yourself time to respond – "I'll get back to you with that information this afternoon."
- Don't forget the tasks that you've agreed to undertake at the meeting; otherwise you'll end up embarrassed at the next one.

ORGANIZING INFORMATION

Businesses produce a massive amount of paper. It is important that these bits of paper are organized – dealt with, stored and capable of being retrieved. While computers have made paper production easier, until they are foolproof they won't make paper documents obsolete. A small sample of the items that need filing by a business include: copies of invoices, purchase orders, contracts, packing slips, time cards, minutes and memos. These all need to be filed in their own special place where you can put your finger on them. Large companies have whole departments that process and file one type of document such as accounts payable or accounts receivable, but you may have to do all of it yourself unless you hire someone to help. The importance of organized filing cannot be over-emphasized. One comment often heard in business is "I hate paper work," but paperwork remains essential.

Consider the following example: You sell a product to the XYZ Company. The product is delivered to XYZ, but your delivery person forgets to give a copy of the packing slip to the receptionist. Your slip is returned to your office and piled up with some other miscellaneous documents. Some time later, your customer receives an invoice from you for the shipment. Their accounts payable department cannot locate the packing slip which they require to issue a cheque. When the cheque does not arrive as you expected, you call XYZ to complain. They politely explain that they were unable to approve the invoice since they could not confirm the delivery of the shipment. They require a copy of the packing slip. Your packing slip was thrown in a pile of miscellaneous documents with a lot of other invoices, packing slips, purchase orders and other sundry documents. The pile became so large and untidy that you thought it might be a good idea to stash it away in a drawer. You can't quite remember which drawer you put it in, but you promise the XYZ accounts payable department that you will fax them a copy of the packing slip. Two hours later you retrieve it from your drawer and fax it over. You'll finally get your cheque – but what a waste of time!

If the delivery person had given the receptionist, receiving clerk or whomever the packing slip at the time of delivery, you would not have to waste time providing a copy. Likewise, if you had a systematized method of filing, it would have taken a few seconds to put your hand on the packing slip. Small business people do not have time to waste.

The two most common ways of storing information are as paper documents and as computer files. Paper documents are filed in metal filing cabinets, file drawers in desks or bankers boxes. All of these are available at office supply stores. No matter how small your business, it will accumulate more files as time passes. Four-drawer filing cabinets are the most commonly used. Within in each drawer you may further subdivide files by using hanging file folders that will hold a number of files.

Computers are excellent for storing large amounts of information and most businesses store a certain amount of information on them although it is not yet possible to eliminate paper records altogether. Some business people claim that computers actually generate more paper than in pre-computer times. Computers are also subject to hard-drive failure and viruses that can destroy information, so regular backing up of files is essential.

SYSTEMS AND FORMS

One way to maintain order is to have procedures and routines. Business forms are an important part of staying organized and keeping records. Here are some common procedures used in business and the forms connected to them:

Sales transactions Cash is taken from a customer and a receipt is given, either handwritten on numerically sequenced forms or produced by a cash register. Copies of receipts are retained for the businesses records. If a mistake is made when writing the receipt, the receipt is voided but retained for balancing purposes. If a mistake is made ringing a sale in on a cash register it must be noted on the cash register tape. Most cash registers have an access window to make notations on the tape. Refunds and credits may be noted the same way. If the payment is given by cheque, it is normal to write the customer's personal information on the back of the cheque. There are rubber stamps available that provide a handy format for the different kinds of information you may require from your customer. If you have a credit card machine, the company you are using will provide an information kit on how to control the use of it. The systematization of the handling of payments in an over-the-counter type of operation is important, especially if you are relying on someone else to do this for you.

Closing off a cash register Depending on the complexity of the cash register, various totals may be rung off on the register tape. The simplest is an overall total. All the cash, cheques and credit card slips are removed from the register and placed in a bag with the cash receipts or register tape. A small predetermined amount of cash, called the "float" is left in the register to start the next day's business. Someone in a quiet place prepares a cash report and subsequently a deposit from the contents of the bag. Any problems in the handling of cash will show up quickly if the cash report or deposit does not balance.

Purchase orders Unless you have an open account with a supplier, your business will probably have to issue purchase orders to obtain supplies and services. A purchase order is a mini contract. The name of your company, the date, the name of the other company, the details of the order and payment terms are all included in a purchase order. Once you have prepared a purchase order and signed it, the order is sent to the other party for signature; then a contractual arrangement exists between the two parties. If your business does a lot of transactions with a certain company for the same product, you may wish to issue an open purchase order. An **open purchase order** is issued once and defines the charges, payment terms and any other relevant issues for future orders. Subsequent orders need only refer to the number of the open purchase order. This saves time and also controls the details of the order.

Since the terms of a purchase order are legally binding, make sure that your final approval is required before they are sent out. Purchase orders are normally prepared in multiple copies, one for your own files, one for the other companies files, and extra copies for incidental parties such as accountants, bookkeepers or other relevant parties in remote locations from your office. Printing companies manufacture triplicate purchase order forms or you may wish to purchase generic purchase orders at office supply stores. You may also create and print out your own purchase orders on a desktop computer.

SAMPLE PURCHASE ORDER

ACME CHEESE CO.

R.R.#2, Blyth, Ontario N0M 1H0
(519) 555-1234 • Fax (519) 555-5678 • E-mail: office@cheeseco.ca

PURCHASE ORDER

PURCHASE ORDER NO: #00001

DATE: Sept. 30, 2001

SHIP TO:
Acme Cheese
Contact: Joe

TO:
Jim's Repair Shop
RR #2
Blyth, ON N0M 1B0

DATE TO ARRIVE	SHIPPING METHOD	TAXABLE ☐ Yes ☐ No	TERMS 30 days

Item	Quantity	Description	Price	Amount
1		Repair	200.00	$ 200.00

Subtotal	$200.00
GST@7%	$ 14.00
TOTAL	$214.00

Contracts and letters of agreement The use of purchase orders is normally reserved for relatively small amounts of payment. It is customary to use a formal contract for large amounts, though the less formal letter of agreement, signed by both parties, is sometimes used if the parties wish to avoid a formal, legal document. The reason smaller amounts are handled differently is that preparing and issuing a contract, or writing up a letter of agreement, is a fair amount of work. The expense of preparing a contract is only justified when the order is quite large or of a continuing nature.

The contents of a contract are the same as a purchase order but more detailed. Since the amounts are greater in a contract and the difficulties greater if there is a problem, make sure a knowledgeable party reviews a contract before you sign it. Your lawyer is the best person for this.

There are three basic elements to a contract:

1) an offer from one individual or company to another to perform a specific act;
2) the acceptance by the other party of the terms of the offer;
3) payment for completing the terms of the contract; this is usually payment of money, but it may sometimes be a promise to do something or not to do something.

An extra element, for contracts in real estate and in some other areas, is a set amount of time within which the terms of the contract are to be completed.

A contract exists when one party makes an offer to perform or refrain from performing a specified act and the other party accepts. A contract is not valid if the terms involve an illegal, immoral or criminal purpose or are against public policy. Some contracts such as real estate transactions must be in writing. Although it is possible for two parties to have a verbal contract, this form is not advisable for a small business person. Any contracts related to your business should be written.

A contract is complete when its terms have been met or when special circumstances arise such as the death of one of the parties. The failure to carry out the terms of a contract (a breach) provides for one party to recoup losses. If the parties to a contract do not agree on how to terminate a breached contract, they may have to turn to the courts to provide a resolution.

If you are entering into a contract, rely on your lawyer to make sure you understand the terms. It is a common practice in business to read over each clause of the terms of a contract separately, sometimes to initial each one.

Invoices

Once you have provided a service or product to a customer, you will want to bill for it. This is done on an invoice form. The information on an invoice form will commonly include your company name, a sequential invoice number, the date, a purchase order number (if available), details of the goods or service supplied, the amount due, terms of payment and any discount available for early payment.

It is important to send invoices out in a timely fashion since an approved invoice generates a cheque. If you are invoicing for goods which were delivered, you should enclose a copy of the packing slip with an invoice. As with purchase orders and other business forms you may have a printing company produce them for you, or you may purchase them at an office supply, or create them on a desktop computer.

SAMPLE SERVICE INVOICE FORM

JIM'S
REPAIR

1001 Jones Road, Winnipeg, Manitoba P3V V3B
Tel. (204) 555-1234 Fax (204) 555-4321

INVOICE# 000001
SALES PERSON: Joe

SERVICE FOR:
Acme Cheese Ltd
RR # 2
Blyth, ON N0M 1B0

INVOICE DATE: Sept. 30, 2001
JOB NAME/NUMBER: 01-8-312

BILL TO: above

Qty	Parts Description	Price	Amount
2	Cheese mixer flanges	40.00	$ 80.00
		Parts Subtotal	$ 80.00

Service person	Labor Description	Hours	Rate
Joe	Install and adjust cheese mixer flanges	2	$ 60.00
		Labor Subtotal	$120.00

We thank you for your business

Subtotal	$200.00
GST@7%	$ 14.00
TOTAL	$214.00

SAMPLE PRODUCT INVOICE FORM

ACME CHEESE CO.

R.R.#2, Blyth, Ontario N0M 1H0
(519) 555-1234 • Fax (519) 555-5678 • E-mail: office@cheeseco.ca

INVOICE # 00001

INVOICE DATE: Sept. 30, 2001

SOLD TO:

ORDER NO.: 100001

TERMS: 30 Days

SALES PERSON Maria

SHIPPED VIA Acme

SHIPPED TO:

F.O.B. N/A

Qty	Description	Price	Amount
15	Cases of Old Cheddar	30.00	$450.00

Subtotal	$450.00
GST@7%	$ 31.50
PST@8%	$ 38.52
FREIGHT	Incl.
Total Due:	$520.02

We thank you for your business

Shipping and Receiving When sending a shipment, make a record of the quantity and condition of the goods. This amount is written on a form called a packing slip and whoever delivers the shipment is expected to get the slip signed and returned to you.

If your business receives shipments, it is your responsibility to check the quantity and condition of the shipment. Any discrepancies or damage may be marked on the packing slip before it is signed. Another form common when shipping and receiving is a bill of lading. This form is used by companies that specialize in the transportation of goods, such as trucking firms and courier services. The bill of lading confirms the date and time of pickup and delivery and may detail the size and weight of the shipment which in turn affect the cost of delivery.

Transmittal forms Some companies that ship information or documents use a form called a transmittal form. The transmittal form or letter functions in the same way as a packing slip: it lists items shipped and serves as a file for future reference. The difference between a packing slip and a transmittal form is that items sent with a transmittal form usually are not followed up with an invoice. The following is sample of a typical packing slip.

ACME CHEESE CO.

R.R.#2, Blyth, Ontario N0M 1H0
(519) 555-1234 • Fax (519) 555-5678 • E-mail: office@cheeseco.ca

PACKING SLIP No. 555555

REFERENCE TO PURCHASE ORDER #

SHIPPED TO:

DATE:

QUANTITY:

RECEIVED BY: DATE:

Inventory control Businesses that depend the sale of products usually keep a stock of goods on hand. This is called inventory. The volume of sales a business may achieve is dependent on how much inventory can be carried in the business at one time and how many times that inventory can be sold. The number of times your complete inventory can be sold is called "turns." For example, if one hundred thousand dollars of inventory represents as much stock as you can have on hand at any particular time, and it takes you all year to sell it, that is one turn. If you sell twice as much, it means you had to fill your inventory twice, therefore you have had two turns. The trick to optimizing inventory turns is to keep your business stocked by re-ordering continually. A great help to knowing how much stock is on hand is an inventory control system.

One inventory control system might work like this: goods come into the receiving department (in many small businesses this is the back door), they are checked off for quantity and entered into an inventory book or ledger. If the business has many types of merchandise it is a good idea to categorize items within the ledger. A code may be assigned to each item to simplify the searching of a particular item. A system is in place, perhaps a two-part price tag, so that when an piece of merchandise is sold one part of the tag is retained. The information on the tags is used to record a sale in the inventory ledger, this reduces the amount of stock shown in the inventory. The inventory list may be reviewed from time to time and orders placed accordingly.

Inventory lists are also used to indicate how much "shrinkage" a business is experiencing. The amount of merchandise physically on hand in a business should match the amount in the inventory book. Differences in these amounts may be caused by sloppy bookkeeping, a break down in your inventory control system or by shoplifting or pilfering.

Some businesses that use a lot of equipment, such as construction companies, need to keep track of equipment especially if it is being moved around regularly. Inventory lists are a great way of doing this. As with merchandise, equipment is entered onto the inventory list when purchased and removed when worn out, broken or stolen.

Cheques Some small business owners get so busy that they delegate the preparing and signing of cheques to someone else. This can be risky. It may be fine to have someone like a bookkeeper or office manager prepare a cheque, but it is advisable to reserve signing cheques to yourself. Your cheque book may provide carbon copies of cheques or a stub which is retained in the cheque book. If your cheque book has a stub section, make sure you fill in all the details such as date, the recipient and the amount, and running balance. This can be useful information at a later date. It is also wise to reserve the review of the monthly bank statement for yourself. That way, you will be able to confirm that the details on the returned cheques match the ones you wrote and balance the statement against your running balance. These may later be forwarded to your bookkeeper or accountant for further review and recording in ledgers.

Making it work

If you have employees whom you expect to adhere to systems, forms and policies it is wise to set up meetings to convey your wishes. Employees respond well to policies and procedures if the logic behind their implementation is explained. Your expectations should be presented in a firm manner, so that there is no question about how you expect things to be done. Verbal instructions should be followed up with written memos or manuals. Staff meetings are also a good place to get feedback from your employees about existing procedures, after all they are the ones who work with them.

As you operate your business you can fine tune your procedures and policies and accumulate them in a manual. Operations manuals are an effective way to bring new employees up-to-speed quickly and provide a set of policies for future reference.

CHAPTER NINE

Employees

The first employee of your small business is you, and chances are that you'll be very demanding of *that* employee, and expect far more of yourself that you would of anyone else. But at some point, every business takes on a second employee ... and then a third ... and suddenly there's an entire personnel group. Without doubt, one of the most vexing problems for small businesses is finding the right people, hiring them, keeping them on track and eliminating undesirable employees. But unless you can do *everything* yourself (and it's often foolish to try), you need to understand how to hire and deal with employees.

There are several possible options when hiring employees. Each should be considered according to the needs of your business.

- Regular, full-time employees who are paid a wage or salary.
- Part-time employees, often used by restaurants or retail stores.
- Temporary or seasonal employees, if your business needs help some times of the year, but not others.
- Sub-contract employees, who work for you and other companies and invoice you for their services.

If you hire someone as an employee you automatically have a payroll. Most employees are paid weekly or bi-weekly. A bi-weekly payroll will save costs since you are doing half the amount of paperwork for the same amount of employee labor. Regardless of the period of payroll or the method of payment (banks will make an automatic deposit, if you request this), here is a list of typical financial obligations that the average employer pays.

Hiring your own

As a small business person, you are now permitted to hire members of your own family to work at your enterprise, provided that they are reasonably paid and you treat them - in accounting terms - exactly as you would any other employee. Usually this means a regular paycheque, deductions for income tax, pension, Employment Insurance, WCB and vacation pay and a T4 at the end of the business year.

PAYROLL DEDUCTIONS

All regular employees and most temporaries must have **personal income taxes** deducted at the source - that means from the paycheque you write for an employee - and remitted to Revenue Canada. The actual rate of deduction varies with income and follows tables supplied by Revenue Canada.

For **Employment Insurance**, the employer contributes the same amount as the employee. An information packet from Revenue Canada will show you exactly how much to deduct and explain when it must be sent to the government.

Employers are also required to pay their employees **vacation pay** when they are on vacation, often 4 percent of the yearly pay. Actual vacation pay is either a period designated by law or an extended amount of vacation negotiated between you and your employee.

Workers' Compensation Boards are set up to provide income to workers in the event of injury and thereby prevent lawsuits against you. The WCB collects premiums from employers and processes payments to injured workers. These are calculated by the WCB for different categories of work on an hourly basis or per hundred dollars of pay. For example, if an employee is paid $300, and the WBC rate for that employee is $2.00 per hundred, the payment by the employer would then be $6.00.

Once you start an account with the WCB you may be asked to provide an estimate of your annual payroll. You will be billed accordingly, therefore it is wise not to overstate your payroll. The WCB reviews your account annually and adjusts your premiums according to your actual past year and your estimate of the next year. It is important to stay on top of this calculation or you may receive unnecessarily high premium notices.

REGULATIONS

Occupational, Health and Safety Acts (usually referred to as OHSA) are in effect in each province across Canada. These regulations define what is expected of employers to protect the health of employees. Some businesses have special regulations for certain higher-risk industries. Get a copy of the appropriate regulations for your business from the local provincial government book store, and abide by it. A violation of the OHSA regulations is a serious matter and may lead to court actions, fines and legal costs.

SELF-EMPLOYED, CONTRACT WORKERS

One way to avoid the cost and bother of payroll deductions is to sub-contract work to individuals who are considered self-employed. The legal requirement is that such workers must be employed by other companies from time to time, and provide their own equipment when working (otherwise they would simply be regular employees of your company).

Contract employees may sometimes appear to be more expensive than payroll employees, but when all the costs are totaled they may better suit your company's needs. Certainly there is less paperwork and more flexibility in arranging for their work. On the other hand, contract employees may not always be available when you most need them, nor can you make the same demands upon them that you would upon full-time employees.

Many small businesses limit the use of contract employees to certain skilled areas - advertising, publications, agenting, computer set-up, engineering, accounting, bookkeeping and similar functions. There is no sense using such employees to sell products in a retail store or do manufacturing work.

PART-TIME AND SEASONAL EMPLOYEES

The use of part-time employees has become increasingly popular since the cost of having such workers on the payroll is usually lower than what would be paid to a full-time employee. Part-time employees are also a good source of help to small businesses which are not large enough to have full-timers on staff. Part-time work is an important part of our economy: it gives students the opportunity to get their first job and gives groups who do not wish to work full-time, such as homemakers and seniors, a source of income.

Some businesses operate differently at different times of the year. Agriculture is most obviously affected by the weather. Other seasonally operated businesses are exterior construction, oil drilling, garden centers and tourism. If you start a business that operates seasonally make sure you know where you are going to get your help.

Casual labor is temporary, part-time work that is done by workers who do not appear on your payroll. They are paid a lump sum and no payroll contributions are made by your company or the worker. An accountant can advise you on how much casual labor Revenue Canada will allow on your books. The usual sources of casual labor are "Temp" services or agencies. These services offer an "all-in" package whereby the employees' payroll costs are included in a lump sum amount paid by you to the agency. Many "temps" eventually become full-time employees at the firms where they have been assigned to work.

HOW TO HIRE

Hiring is one of the most stressful experiences for anyone in business. No matter how much time and care is taken, there is no guarantee that an employee will work out. However, unless care is taken, it is almost certain that a new-hire will turn out to be a personnel disaster.

Some small businesses have found that having employees recommended by associates or other employees is effective. Other employers advertise a position in the newspaper and interview prospective employees who respond. A few small businesses use the services of Canada Manpower, especially for students over the summer vacation. If it is difficult to fill a certain position a business may retain a "head-hunter," an employment consultant who will find the right candidate for a position. Head-hunters work for a fee which is often the equivalent of three or four months wages, but can be as much as a year's salary for recruiting a top-level executive.

Before you place the newspaper ad or make the phone call to a recommended candidate, you'll need to work out a **hiring procedure**. The job should be carefully specified in advance, an exercise which should help you arrive at a written **job description**. You must also decide how you want to sort out applicants. A newspaper ad could produce hundreds of people who want a job with your company. Do you want a résumé from each of them? A list of references? How many people are you prepared to interview? And when the interviews take place, what are you going to ask?

If you do not have a lot of experience interviewing people, it may be useful to write out a list of questions that will be asked of each candidate. After the interview, it is always wise to call references to check on the accuracy of the information you received. It is important to remember that it is much more expensive and time-consuming to fire a bad employee than it is to hire a good one.

Once a person is hired, there should be a probationary period of three months before the person is taken on as a permanent member of your staff.

HOW TO EVALUATE

Once a person begins working for your company, you should keep track of items such as attendance, tardiness, attitude, ambition, trustworthiness, special accomplishments and ability to learn. It is a good idea to sit down with employees periodically to discuss their performance. Some businesses evaluate their employees at the beginning of the year, and use the results when considering pay increases and promotions. A fair evaluation process protects your company from possible "wrongful dismissal" suits.

Aside from laws that prohibit discrimination and harassment in the workplace, it is a good idea to treat employees as you would want to be treated if you were in their place. Remember, as an employer, you are responsible for how your employees behave towards one another. Create a policy for personnel and make each employee aware of it. Be consistent. If you have a particularly valuable employee, make sure you reward that person accordingly. Likewise, if you have a particularly non-productive employee, do yourself and the employee a favor and terminate them.

If managing employees becomes a large part of your business, you might want to take a community college or university course in business, personnel or "organizational behavior" to better understand how to motivate and organize your workforce.

HOW TO FIRE

Many small business owners believe that they can dismiss an employee whenever they wish. But if they do so, and have not followed the proper steps, they may end up facing a wrongful dismissal lawsuit. One way to avoid this result when terminating an employee is to have a system of progressive discipline in place. One system might go like this: each time an employee is guilty of a serious infraction of your company policy, a letter is placed in the employee file. Your employee is made aware of this letter and given a chance to respond in writing. If an employee has two letters on file within a given period, he or she is given a formal warning. When a third infraction occurs, the employee is dismissed.

Of course, employees must be aware of your disciplinary policy. If it becomes necessary to terminate a person's employment, it is best to do it early in the week and early in the day. The reasons for termination should be prepared ahead, and be absolutely clear. All pay, including vacation pay, should be ready the day of termination and any forms required by the government should be filled out ahead of the termination interview. Firing is never a pleasant part of doing business, but it is a necessary one. Employers who shy away from terminating poor employees discourage their good workers and will ultimately cripple their businesses.

CHAPTER TEN

Your workplace

WORKING OUT OF YOUR HOME

Small businesses have been run from homes for centuries. Before the industrial revolution of the 18th century, most products and services were provided by cottage industries. It is ironic that in the late 20th century we are returning to an old-fashioned way of working.

Even before the recent popularity of home offices, certain businesses were traditionally run from homes such as doctors, architects and consultants offices. For these, and other small businesses, there are some tremendous benefits to operating a business at or from your home:

- You do not pay rent or lease costs.
- You do not commute. This reduces wear and tear on vehicles; it also saves time which can be used more effectively either in your business or with your family.
- You can start and finish work when you choose. Small business people frequently work late nights and weekends, but can reward themselves by taking off a mid-week afternoon for golf.
- For tax purposes, you may write off a portion of your mortgage interest or rent, and your house expenses against your business income.

Of course, there are disadvantages as well. A part of your house will be taken over by your business, so you'll have that much less room to live in. If you have small children, they may not understand that the business computer is "off limits" or that mom and dad are really "working" when they're in the home office. And not every small business person can mentally divide "working" at home from "being" at home - which can make work less efficient.

Nonetheless, almost every small business starts in the home, even if just to save some start-up cash. Areas of house that you might consider for an office might be the attic, a spare bedroom, a family room, den or a part of your basement. Garages can easily be converted into offices or workshops. You may ultimately spend eight or more hours a day in your home workplace, so some effort should be taken to make sure it is attractive and comfortable.

Make your home office livable

- If possible, use a ground floor or upper level rather than the basement. It will be more comfortable for you and your customers, if and when they visit your place of business.
- Spend a little money to decorate your work area. Use bright, cheery colors. Hang a few framed prints or posters. Keep the space lean and uncluttered.
- Try to locate your office in a room with a view. You're the boss - you deserve it.
- Get a separate phone line for your business. You don't want your three-year-old taking calls from major corporate clients.
- Create a business feeling and you're more likely to make your home office a business place.

RENTING OR LEASING A WORKPLACE

Some businesses, such as a stores or restaurants, cannot be run from a home; and some home businesses quickly outgrow a home base. In other circumstances, you may find that a home base does not offer sufficient prestige, or isolation from the family, to be an effective place for you to work. Once you have more than one employee, it becomes very difficult to work from your home. So when you're ready, it's time to consider a rented or leased workplace.

Leasing versus Renting It is foolhardy for a business to rent a property on a month-to-month basis. The time effort and investment to establish a business in a location is wasted if you're given notice to vacate a property. However unfair this may seem, landlords are within their rights doing this: businesses are not protected by landlord-tenant legislation. Small business owners can avoid this danger by signing a lease with a landlord for a specific length of time.

A **lease** is a contract between a landlord (the **lessor**) and a tenant (the **lessee**) to occupy certain premises. A lease will spell out terms of the occupancy. Once a lease has been signed by both parties, it is a legally binding document. The tenant is said to have an **interest** in the property for the length of the lease. The following are some items commonly found in leases:

- The names of the tenant and landlord.
- The amount to be paid. This is usually expressed as so much per square foot. Square footage is calculated from the space enclosed by the interior walls.
- The period of payment (usually monthly).
- How long the tenant will occupy the property. Common periods of occupancy are three and five years although any period might be specified. A small business owner must carefully decide how long to commit to paying a lease and how long you intend to do business in a given location.
- Options for renewal. Most commercial leases contain provisions for the tenant to renew the lease at a set terms for a specified amount of time. Leases that include renewal options are sometimes described as "five and five." This means five years for the first term of the lease and an optional term of five years should you choose to renew.
- How much the tenant will contribute to the overall maintenance of the building (common area costs).
- Whether taxes are paid by the tenant or the landlord.
- Whether a percentage of the tenants sales will paid to the landlord (this is common in mall locations).

You may hear terms such as net lease, net-net lease, or triple-net lease used when speaking to landlords or real estate agents. This refers to the inclusion or exclusion of various items in leases and may be explained simply. In a **net lease**, the tenant pays an all-inclusive amount that covers taxes, common area expenses, utilities and any other items specific to the particular property being leased. With a **net-net lease,** the tenant pays the property taxes themselves. Taxes may vary from year to year, and landlords use this kind of lease to avoid unknown increases in costs. With a **triple-net lease** the tenant pays a base rent, plus taxes, plus common area costs. This is the type of lease used by owners of large commercial properties such as malls. Sometimes a percentage of the tenant's sales may make up a portion of or all of the monthly payment. **Percentage leases** include a clause allows the landlord to confirm the volume of sales through access to the your books. In addition, the hours of operation and the level of maintenance of the property may be specified. The signage on the exterior of the building may be restricted, especially in a mall location. If you're fortunate, the landlord may pay an allowance for you to make improvements or by fixtures for the property.

When there is a glut of vacant commercial properties on the market, you will often be able to negotiate favorable terms in a lease, such as a period of no rent, a graduated payment schedule, or payment of leasehold improvements by the landlord. When commercial space is at a premium such as during an economic boom, it becomes difficult to get any concessions from landlords.

There is no such thing as an oral contract in real estate law, therefore all leases must be written, signed, dated and witnessed. Since leases are complex legal documents, don't sign one until a lawyer has reviewed it. You may also wish to consult an accountant about the financial aspects of a lease.

THE INSTANT OFFICE

The start-up expense of leasing an office discourages some people from moving a small business out of their home. One solution to this is offered by companies who provide work space to small businesses for a fee. If your business needs to operate from an office, but you're unsure about the longevity of your operation, this is a great way to avoid the expense of leasing or building an office. The service these companies offer is called "packaging."

Companies that offer packages own or lease large spaces in commercial buildings. This space is then divided into work areas or offices which are, in turn, rented or leased to individual businesses. Sometimes the types of businesses are restricted to a single industry. Often, a variety of services are included in a monthly fee. These might include a telephone line, a receptionist, photocopiers, fax machines and computers, and other sundry business needs. These resources are shared with the other tenants in the complex.

RETAIL SPACES

Always remember the first three rules of retail - LOCATION! LOCATION! LOCATION! Location is always a factor when establishing a business, but the importance of location varies from one business to another.

Businesses that rely on a portion of their sales from walk-in traffic are most affected by choice of location. Two business that are especially affected by location choice are retail stores and restaurants. If your small business should fall into these categories, be sure to consider the following when choosing a retail space:

Traffic The number of people and cars that pass the location per day is called traffic. Business experience shows that if you have a large flow of pedestrian or vehicular traffic going by your place of business, a certain percentage will come in to shop or dine regardless of other factors. There are companies that will do a traffic survey of a location for a fee. Some landlords have this done to show potential tenants how much traffic to expect.

Other neighboring businesses Some businesses are "destinations" and customers will go out of their way to do business there. Locating near a "destination" business will give you the benefit of their flow of customers. The fact that there may be the same kind of businesses as yours in the immediate area is not necessarily a bad thing. Some business neighborhoods become known for a specific industry, like fashion, lighting or fabrics. Each individual business can attract customers for different reasons such as price point, quality or selection.

Vacant premises An area with a great many vacancies should ring alarm bells. This could mean that the area is a place where it is difficult to stay in business. On the other hand, properties in these neighborhoods can be rented cheaply, sometimes just to cover the landlords costs. If your business draws customers independently, the success or failure of other businesses may not matter that much.

Overall trends Neighborhoods go through phases, and developers try to buy properties when they are run down and can be bought cheaply. The idea is to improve the properties to the point where they can demand higher rents, therefore producing an exceptional return on the initial investment. Smart retailers know this and try to get in on the trend before the rents go up.

Parking You may have the best looking store, the greatest selection, the lowest prices, or the best service - but if your customers can't find a place to park near your store, you will have a problem.

Proximity to suppliers and customers The distance from your suppliers may affect the cost of delivery. Likewise, if delivery is part of a service you offer customers, you may have to consider how far your business is located from the market you are servicing. Service businesses that operate from a base and regularly go out to customers homes or businesses must consider the location of the base to their customers.

Prestige In some cities, the prestige of certain locations may justify exorbitant rents. If you expect to serve high-end customers or clients at a high-end billing rate, you may well need a prestigious office.

Working out of your vehicle

Some business people spend a majority of their working day in a vehicle. An answering service, a mobile phone and a laptop computer with a modem allow these people to do most of their business on the road. This is truly a "virtual office." If it turns out to be your office just be sure your car has a good coffee mug holder.

COMPUTERS FOR YOUR OFFICE

Computers can now be used to handle many functions that used to be done by individual employees. While they won't brew you a cup of coffee, they are capable of handling many business activities:

THE PROGRAM	*WHAT IT DOES FOR A SMALL BUSINESS*
Accounting	Maintain electronic ledgers, prepare payroll, prepare income tax, write cheques.
Word processing	Create and print letters, envelopes, faxes, E-mail and memos.
Desktop publishing	Create flyers, business cards, brochures, press releases and calendars.
Spreadsheet	Handle accounting, automatic number calculations, compare and correlate information.
Database	Store and retrieve information such as customer names, contact lists, phone numbers and employee information.
CAD	Create plans, sketches, drawings.
Fax modem	Replaces a fax machine.
Telephone modem	Replaces an answering service or receptionist.

Because a computer is so central to small business filing and record-keeping, it's important that the hardware and software be relatively up-to-date and that its files be backed up regularly. A computer crash is no excuse if Revenue Canada decides to audit your company or a customer wants to know what happened to her order.

MAILING AND SHIPPING

Even with the advent of couriers, faxes and E-mail, Canada Post is still the most important resource for small businesses. The range of services provide by Canada Post that might be useful to a small business include post office boxes, flyer delivery, registered mail, express delivery and plain old postal delivery. If you need a lot of postage in your business you may want to invest in a postage meter. This saves time spent lining up at the post office.

There are some private businesses that mirror the services offered by Canada Post; the main advantage of these businesses is the convenience of their location. They actually provide the mail-room functions found in large corporations to small businesses.

Faxing and E-mailing have altered the way businesses communicates, and there are cost savings in both methods. There are still some problems with the security and efficacy of these systems, but since they are so important to business it is only a matter of time until they are sorted out.

CHAPTER ELEVEN

Growing your small business

If you are successful in your business there will be a natural tendency for the business to grow. To the individual who is just starting out, future concerns over the extent of growth may seem pointless. But the fact is that many businesses, which are successful at start-up, fail when they grow too fast or too large. The reasons behind this phenomenon are complex, however there are some points to consider when your business begins to grow.

Size Initially, most small business owners have a hands-on knowledge of their operation. The bigger the business gets, the harder it becomes to know what is going on. One problem that many small businesses experience when they grow quickly is control of cash flow - how much cash is coming into the business and how much is going out. Systems set up to handle a certain amount of cash flow often do not work effectively when the volume increases. An accountant or banker appropriate for a relatively low volume of business may be inappropriate for a higher volume of business. A set of employees who could handle the business last year may be swamped by incoming orders next year. A smart small business person has to stay on top of growth and change the business operation accordingly.

Workforce Even though a business may have the opportunity to grow, the workforce to accomplish that growth may not be available. This is especially true when the workers are skilled. The use of unskilled workers where skilled labor is required is a recipe for disaster. If you can't get the kind of workers you need, make an active choice not to expand.

Keep a life!

There is a tendency for any small business to become an all-consuming passion. This may be very good for your fledgling business, but it can be lousy for your relationship with a spouse, with your children and with your old friends. If you start forgetting your kids' names and your spouse's birthday, or you can't remember the last time you took a day off work, it's time for a pause. A small business should enhance your life, not take it over.

Administrative structure Some companies get bigger for the simple reason that they need more people to get the work done. More people means more payroll, more scheduling for vacations and more filling-in for sick time. The more people on staff, the more people are need to manage them.

Another item to consider is the increase in the accounting load. More business means more invoices, packing slips, statements, cheques, deposits, etc. It is important to be able to justify an increase in profit before adding administrative costs.

Management When a business grows, it goes through predictable changes in management structure. The first phase may be characterized by the owner who knows everything that goes on in the company and has a hand in all decisions. The second phase may include a level of middle managers who manage the staff beneath them and report directly to the owner. The third phase is where the owner takes on a role such as chief executive officer and has an executive level of management.

Unfortunately, the process of growth in a company does not always follow such a sequential pattern of change in management. For example, a company may have one part of the operation run by a vice president with a group of middle managers and another part of the operation run by a middle manager reporting to the owner.

Businesses often feel growing pains when parts of the operation are functioning ineffectively due to improper levels of management. The problem many small companies face is hiring the right people to manage larger operations.

A company with zero growth will not stay in business long. Even the smallest of businesses must grow to some extent, otherwise it will not be able to survive a downward fluctuation in volume. The two greatest challenges a company faces when growing is how to find the right staff and where to get the money to finance growth. Once these questions are resolved, the possibility still remains that a larger company won't continue to be fun for you, the owner. This is why many entrepreneurs - after creating a successful business - sell that operation to others and go back to what they enjoy most - starting *another* small business.

NOTES & UPDATES

NOTES & UPDATES